Hardscrabble Featherbed

By Marilyn McNew Core

ISBN: 978-1-09831-756-0

CONTENTS

FOREWORD

Everyone has a story to tell, and I wanted to write mine down for my family and friends to keep as a reference guide of a time more than half a century ago, when things were simpler. Things were simpler, but often, just making ends meet was a formidable task and days, weeks, months, and even years would pass with more of the same. These are my memories of that time. Some of them may not be as accurate as others would recall, but this is how I remember them, and it is my story. In today's time, being politically correct is a huge issue and I will admit that after I proofread my stories, I changed some of the sentences because I was afraid I might hurt someone's feelings. There were some things, which happened, that I chose to leave out because they may have brought up unpleasant memories to the individuals involved, and I surely would not want that! If you are listed by name, please know that you are a special memory from my childhood and I thank you for being present in my life. I chose the title of these stories to be <u>Hardscrabble Featherbed</u> because although I slept on a soft featherbed, life was, at best, hardscrabble.

Gratitude tugs at me to mention the families which are clearest in my memories and to whom I will always be thankful. These families: Ayers, Bailey, Capps, Daniels, Davis, Flowers, Fortner, Griffin, Hall, Hill, Holley, Johnson, McClellan, Mears, Morgan, Nichols, Sammon, Shivers, Shoupe, Skipper, Stone, Pitts, Rainey, Taylor, Walden and Yon; thank you for your influence and support during my growing up years.

DEDICATION

When I first began writing this book, my beautiful and talented daughter, Candy, was still very much alive. She encouraged me to write and always showed approval of my offerings, however humble or less than stellar they were. Candy was a wonderful writer herself and was extremely pleased to co-author a book of her own for educators, which was published at Region IV where she worked. She never seemed to stop thinking of ways to encourage others, especially educators, whom she was passionate about. Even while undergoing wicked chemotherapy, she would pull out her computer and creatively type away. The day she stopped using her computer was one of the saddest that I have endured. I know she would want everyone to keep "telling their story" as she did so eloquently, and that is why, Candy (Doll), this book is lovingly dedicated to you and all the precious memories you left behind to help us cope with the fact that though we will never see you again on this earth, we will rejoice with you in Heaven someday!

All my love, Mom

Candy Jeris Core

JULY 25, 1974 – JUNE 11, 2011

ACKNOWLEDGEMENTS

Hardscrabble Featherbed would never have existed without the help and encouragement from the special people in my life. Thank you to my son, Jerrod, for patiently scanning all the stories and pictures for the book. Thank you to my husband, Jerry, for supporting me every step of the journey. Thank you to my brother, George, for supplying me with memories and pictures of hardscrabble days. Thank you to my friends Dee and Billy Moore who encouraged me to put my stories on paper. Thanks to my sisters, Sarah and Georgette, brothers George and Bill, and stepmother, A.D., for experiencing living on a fish camp with me. To all the friends and families who lived and/or live in Calhoun County, Florida, my gratitude is endless, for shaping me into the person I am today. I know that Hurricane Michael devastated many of your homes and lands, but I know how strong your spirit is and I know you will rebuild and be even stronger. Thank you!

Marilyn McNew Core

HISTORY OF KINARD

In 1960, the Andy Griffith show debuted on television and I fell in love with the show and the characters. It never occurred to me that Mayberry was a small town because I lived in Kinard (pronounced Ki'nerd). Kinard did not have a traffic light and the main "town" area was Hill's Store on one side of State Highway 73 and Kinard Elementary School on the other side. The rest of the town was made up of neighboring houses and a Pentecostal Holiness Church. Only a few families lived in Kinard around the start of the 1900s, and Kinard was first known as Chafin, Florida, after the elected county judge in 1920, but was later renamed Kinard after a resident, Tom Kinard.

For their livelihood, the residents of Kinard dipped turpentine, logged, ran sawmills, or farmed. The wages for plowing with a mule came to a whopping fifty cents a day. Picking cotton would bring three cents per pound with a free meal and free transportation. A person could make up to $3.50 a week for dipping turpentine. Making a living was hard and some people chose to make moonshine and outwit the "revenoors." Folks supplemented their larder by hunting deer, turkey, or other game and by fishing.

Supplies that could not be grown had to be bought from Blountstown, a town eighteen miles away, which meant a long trip by mule and wagon. Some people chose to get their staples, which came in barrels floated down the river on boats, to the Oak Grove Landing, which was the nearest fish camp to ours.

People had to "doctor" themselves and get midwives to deliver their babies until the first doctor arrived in Kinard. He had to work by lamplight since REA did not bring electricity into Kinard until 1949. I was born in 1949, but in Panama City, Florida, not Kinard.

MEMORIES OF LONG AGO AND FAR AWAY

Childhood memories surface clearly and long to tell their story.

Listen! Do you hear?

The ebony musty-smelling creek laps gently at the cypress trees.

Fishing boat and poles, red worms and chirping crickets,

An old Maxwell House Coffee can used as a boat bailing vessel,

A rough-hewn wooden paddle slicing silently through the dark water,

Propels a solitary small soul forward toward a large and treacherous lake

Filled with submerged stumps waiting to snag and trap an unskilled boater.

The stumps don't scare Girl.

She paddles swiftly forward seeking a known fishing spot and anchors.

The only noise she hears is the chirr, chirr, chirr of the caged crickets or

The occasional shrill squawking cry

Of the hawk overhead, but it does not bother Girl.

Today is her day to be one with the lake.

More memories speak . . .

Fast forward to Wash Day.

Monday is always Wash Day unless weather does not permit the clothes to be dried.

The white clapboard house shuttered green and surrounded by blue
       hydrangea hedges.

Stands at attention as the plump, white-haired matriarch, Grandma, and Girl

Prepare to wash the clothes.

Boy, who is younger by almost two years, is allowed to play happily,

Excused for now from washing duties because of his age and the fact that

The cranky, old wringer washer can be cantankerous at times.

Girl's two small freckled hands feed the wet clothes through the wringer

Into a galvanized washtub.

Bare feet gingerly sidestepping the piercing sandspurs

And the itchy stinging nettles, those same freckled hands

Hang the washed Cloroxed white sheets in the hot summer sun to dry.

Satisfaction crosses her face with a smile as a gentle breeze

Causes the sheets to billow and flap languidly.

Though the sheets will feel scratchy to the touch,

They will smell sunny and delicious on the featherbed tonight.

Girl's smile lingers on her lips as she observes the pulsating sheets
On the rickety old clothesline.
She is lost in her daydream world again, pirouetting gracefully
Before a large audience.
Grandma is quick to remind Girl that
"Cleanliness is next to Godliness!" just in case she should get any
Fancy addle-brained ideas.
To make sure Girl has heard her,
Grandma adds the part about "Hellfire and Damnation"
Referring to yesterday's sermon preached to the Cypress Creek Missionary Baptist
    Church congregation.
Of which Grandma, Girl, and Boy are proud members.
Girl gets the not too subtle message and wipes the smile from her face.
Resignedly, she turns away from the serenity of the outdoors and enters her home.
It's time to prepare dinner, a meal eaten around noon-time.
Supper was consumed early, around five o'clock in the evening.
Meals were never hurried nor gourmet.
Fried brown hushpuppies and crispy caught-that-morning catfish,
Bacon-seasoned turnip greens and hot crusty cornbread
Or pinto beans and cathead biscuits
These items were the usual fare shared by Grandma, Girl, and Boy.
There would be plates to scrape and wash and the kitchen floor must be swept,
But, sometimes after supper, Girl would open the cedar chest
And let the smells refresh her memories of long ago and far away.
Her mother's satin wedding gown is nestled in its fraying box.
Her father's Navy Seabees's coat is wrapped in tattered tissue paper. The hand cro-
    cheted wedding quilt conceal its secrets in its folds.
Boxes and boxes of old black and white photos
Beckon Girl to inspect them and remember.
The clouds of memory begin to wither and vanish, as Girl,
Who is a woman now, returns to the present modern world.
The woman knows that if the memories dim and fade
She has but to open the battered old cedar chest.
Once again the smells invade her senses
And she savors and remembers the long ago and far away times.

IT TAKES A VILLAGE

It's said that "It takes a village to raise a child!" The village I grew up in was in the Panhandle of Florida, a tiny community named Kinard. It was not unlike the frontier land of the Wild West, uncharted, untouched territory.

The few families who lived in Kinard were hardworking, "salt of the Earth" folks. They lived by their grit, wit and determination, making their living by dipping turpentine, logging, farming, or running sawmills.

The history I mentioned earlier, I learned from doing research so that I could explain how we lived in those years.

Everyone has a story to tell but I wanted to write mine down for my family and friends to keep for a reference guide about a time more than half a century ago, when things were simpler. Things were simpler, but often just making ends meet was a formidable task and days, weeks, months and even years would pass with more of the same. These are my memories of that time. Some of them may not be as accurate as others would recall, but this is how I remember them, and it is my story. I mentioned the names of real people who helped me grow up and to whom I owe much for their interaction in my life. I truly mean to embarrass no one, only to share my memories before they fade away like oak trees surrendering their leaves to the winds of winter. So, here are my memories of growing up in the days of "Hardscrabble Featherbed."

THE "BIG HOUSE" THAT I GREW UP IN

THE FISH CAMP CABINS CIRCA 1950

MOMMA AND AUNT FRANCES AT OUR BOAT LANDING.

EASTER AT THE FISH CAMP 1954

CHAPTER 1

CYPRESS CREEK LODGE-A DESCRIPTION

My father, William Ford McNew, known to most as Bill, was a boilermaker by trade, and obviously, he was good at his job since he was made foreman on most of the jobs which were done in the shipyards. Bill had always done things his way, so when he discovered what would later become Cypress Creek Lodge, he immediately began planning the layout of the camp. He had found and bought the land jointly with his cousin, Fred Peake. The previous owners of the land had eased out a boat landing behind the sawmill that they ran, but everything else was untouched. The nearest town is Wewahitchka, nine miles west, and the beautiful beaches of Panama City lie forty miles west. Our fish camp was literally in the middle of nowhere. But that did not deter my father, who saw the camp as a big draw for fishermen since Cypress Creek fed into the eerily haunting Dead Lakes of Wewahitchka.

Daddy (Bill) kept his day job as a boilermaker but went to work mapping out how he envisioned our fish camp to look. He constructed a "big house" where we would live, three cabins to be rented out, a cook shack, a shower house, a tool shed, a root cellar, wormbeds, a minnow pond, and a boat landing. He also plowed up the land above the boat landing and made a garden there, the rich dark soil being ideal for growing vegetables. For the buildings, Daddy used surplus material obtained from Tyndall Air Force Base circa WWII. Each cabin held two bedrooms with a bathroom between them. The charge for renting was two dollars nightly, and for added convenience, there was an outdoor area where the fishermen could clean their fish. There was also a shower house and a cook shack with wooden stoves and picnic tables. The cook shack was actually two separate kitchens so that more than one guest could cook their meals. And so, Cypress Creek Lodge was up, open and ready for business.

The "big house," where my parents, grandparents, my brother, George and I lived, was originally constructed to serve as a dining hall for clients. Daddy envisioned serving food in the large front area, so as he was building the house, he built in many windows which looked out upon our mimosa trees, sand bed and the highway.

He installed a bathroom that had a single toilet, one bedroom with a small closet, and a large kitchen that had a sink with a pump. My parents, and George and I slept in the bedroom. When my grandparents moved down from Alabama to live with us, Daddy added two beds at the back of the front room, but my grandfather, of his own choice, always slept on a mattress on the floor beside the potbelly stove.

Fishermen did come to our fish camp from Florida and neighboring states of Alabama, Georgia, Mississippi, and Tennessee. They had heard, by word of mouth, that Cypress Creek was a good starting point for catching a record number of fish. Daddy was delighted and created another feature which the fishermen liked. He made three wormbeds and sold the worms for a penny each. My brother, George, and I, usually dug the worms, gray wigglers or smaller red worms, placed them into white cardboard cups, and labeled them. We had to add some of the wormy soil to the cups before capping them so that the fishermen could easily remove the fresh worms to bait their hooks. Daddy loved to fish so if the union was on strike and he was home, he would offer to serve as a guide for the fishermen. He didn't charge for doing this since he loved sharing fish stories and beer with the clients. We never kept a record book of who stayed, but we usually got to know the clients well and became friends with many of them. We kept in touch for years and I have shared some of their stories in this book.

In the next few pages, I have written brief biographies of my grandmother, father, and mother. My grandfather, Wiley Fred McNew, whom we called Dad, I chose not to write about because he passed away one year after my mother died. He was sick for a long time and bedridden so I simply didn't get to know him very well. I didn't write a biography of my brother, George, but I included stories of him. He and I are only eighteen months apart in age. Now we live miles from Cypress Creek Lodge, but it's never far from our minds. George and his family plan to move back to Calhoun County, Florida, and build a home. George helped me with the memories in this book and I am forever grateful for his input.

FOOD FROM THE EARTH

The big house had an even bigger yard and Grandma turned part of it into a vegetable garden.Daddy plowed up the rich black soil near the boat landing for an even bigger garden.

Our gardens were seasonal, and Grandma depended on Poor Richard's Almanac and the Grit Newspaper for tips on when to plant the various vegetables to

11

get maximum growth out of them. In the spring and summer months, we enjoyed Irish potatoes, pole beans, butterbeans, field peas, cucumbers, okra, carrots, squash, onions, watermelons, cantaloupes, tomatoes, and eggplants. Daddy even managed to grow kale, which we used to make a salad, by adding tomatoes and onions. Mayonnaise was the only salad dressing we used. Eating salads didn't seem to be the norm back then unless it was potato salad.

Our fall garden produced turnip, collard and mustard greens. Giant orange pumpkins, with leaves as big as a man's hand, were harvested and made into pies. We always shared our garden's bounty with our neighbors and they shared with us.

We had a persimmon tree and a cumquat tree growing near the big house and both were very productive. I never developed a taste for persimmons, but the cumquats were tasty. I liked to pick and eat the greener cumquats because it seemed they were tangier than the orange/yellow color of the riper fruit.

The Mears family, our nearest neighbors, had pear trees which overflowed year after year with more fruit than they could use, so they always invited us to come and get as many pears as we wanted. We always made sure to pick some extra ripe pears for Mrs. Mears, who was busy raising two boys and two girls and didn't have the time to pick the pears herself. Grandma would take the pears home to make some cobblers, pear preserves, and a jam she called "pear honey." Pear honey was made by combining sweetened boiled pears and canned crushed pineapple. Jars filled with this mixture and canned by the water bath method would sparkle a shiny golden color. Nothing tasted better than pear honey on a buttered biscuit!

In the woods near Oak Grove Fish Camp, about three miles west of our home, Daddy discovered a wild chinquapin tree. Chinquapins are small acorn-like nuts, tasting like a cross between a pecan and a peanut. They were a real treat.

Blackberries grew wild around the fish camp, as did scuppernong grapes. Grandma could easily turn both into jelly, and as a bonus, she would make a blackberry cobbler out of some of the leftover berries.

Some years, we would travel fifty miles east to Telogia because there were fields of blueberries there to be picked. It was hot sticky work picking those green-pea sized blueberries, and there was the added aggravation of swatting mosquitoes and hoping no chigger decided to hide in your pants leg and cause an awful itch! But in the end, it was worth it to carry home enough blueberries for pies and some leftover to freeze.

I think Daddy and Grandma were good stewards of the earth. Vegetables were planted for consumption, fish were caught and game was hunted for the same reason. No frivolous waste, just simple survival tactics for living at that time.

FISH CAMP FLOWERS

I felt this story needed to be added to describe more of what the fish camp looked like in its heyday. Had Grandma not had a green thumb, the fish camp would have been a bleak presence in the pines and oaks of Northwest Florida. But, thank God, Grandma's touch, like King Midas, whose touch turned things to gold, turned plants green. On one side of the big house, she planted a magnolia tree, which was about the same height as me when I was three years old. I grew taller with age, but that magnolia tree flourished and towered over me, giving us many years of large and fragrant blooms. In front of our kitchen where our sink drained, Grandma planted a wisteria vine. It grew and produced purple grape-like clusters of petals and smelled heavenly. Unfortunately, the wisteria vine loved to climb and managed to twine around the tall pine tree that was close by. The wisteria literally choked the pine tree to death, much like a boa constricts its prey. In between the magnolia tree and the wisteria vine, grandma planted gardenia, which thrived and produced sweet-smelling white flowers. Big, blue hydrangeas festooned the front of the big house, and further in front of them, Daddy grew mimosa trees. These trees had beautiful pink flowers but Daddy planted them because mimosa webworm caterpillars infested these trees, and we would pick these caterpillars off for fish bait. They were nasty little creatures, but useful for fishing. We had two large grape vines which provided us with snacks, jellies and jams and plenty was left over to share with our neighbors. A pyracantha bush grew beside the entrance to the wormbeds/rabbit cages and each year its bright red berries would emerge around Christmas time.

Small delicate Cherokee roses grew alongside the power box and bigger pink and red roses grew nearer the big house. When my mother became ill, Daddy planted purple and fuchsia-colored crape myrtles along the sandy driveway to our house since they were my mother's favorite flower. Elephant ears and Easter lilies grew near the old shed and purple verbena and variegated phlox were scattered across our yard. Orange poppies, yellow daylilies, and Johnny Jump-Ups clustered together on a ridge leading to our neighbors' home. Grandma never seemed to tire of weeding and watering all the many plants and flowers, and she was generous about sharing cuttings and bouquets of them. She always sent flowers and bouquets with George and me to Cheryl's mother, Mrs. Walden. Grandma would share cuttings from her flowers with neighbors so they could grow their own and if she saw a flower in a neighbor's yard, she had no qualms about asking for a cutting from it. However, she never said "Thank you" for the cutting because she believed that if thanks were given, the flower would perish. I never knew if this was one of Poor Richard's notions or yet another "Grandmaism." Whatever it was, it seemed to work because Grandma really did have a green thumb!

RABBITS, RED WORMS AND WIGGLERS

On our fish camp, Daddy constructed three wormbeds. A wormbed is a soil-enriched plot of land made to grow and breed worms. The worms were sold to our fish camp visitors to use for fishing in the creek and lake. Red worms were just that—small, soft, pliable red worms which could easily be hooked. Wigglers were larger, grayish, fat and squirmy. They were good for attracting fish because they had more spirit and were livelier. A box of one hundred red worms cost a dollar or a penny per worm.

Wigglers were two cents a worm. George and I had the job of digging these worms, counting them, putting them in the cardboard cups and making sure there was enough soil around them to keep them moist and ready for the fishermen.

Daddy bought rabbits at the feed store in Blountstown, made cages and suspended the rabbits above the two longest wormbeds. In this way, the worms were treated to the rabbit pellets as well as the food that fell through the spaces in the cages. These wormbeds were covered, but the smaller one was not. The smaller wormbed was made of bricks and originally, Daddy had made it to be a pool for us. But, Momma was worried that having a pool with campers around might result in an accidental drowning.

So, Daddy relented and turned the would-be pool into another wormbed. He then added another pump and fish cleaning area for the campers. His tool shed was next to all this, so that his tools were always handy if needed.

FLOUR POWER

Flour, a staple in our house, was sold in ten-pound bags. These sacks were printed with whimsically happy designs of flowers, butterflies and other brightly colored items. Grandma would buy the flour because she needed it for her baking needs. After the flour was used up, Grandma would take the flour sacks apart at the seams, wash the material, and then make blouses for me from it. My blouses were starched and crisply ironed and I don't know if anyone knew, or cared, that they had once been flour sacks. Another bonus provided by the flour was that on occasion, one could get a free dinner plate with the purchase of the flour. Grandma saved those beautiful plates until she had a dozen of them and right about that time, Mr. and Mrs. Monroe Johnson moved into their newly built house and had a house-warming party. The entire community was invited. Grandma bundled and wrapped up the dozen dinner plates and gave them to the Johnsons as a house warming gift. When I would outgrow a flour sack blouse, Grandma would cut it up and make quilt pieces out of it, and when enough pieces were accumulated, she would stitch them together in quilt squares, and make a quilt top. Eventually, she would join the quilt top to the batting and a quilt bottom and my flour sack blouses would live again as a covering for my bed. Although Grandma never heard the slogan, "Reduce. Reuse. Recycle," she lived it daily.

THE READING TREE

My mother was an avid reader and when she passed away; her books remained in her room.

Grandma wasn't sure whether I should read some of them because they were adult novels. But reading had opened a whole new world for me, and I was eager to read any and every book I could find. So, I started reading my mother's books when I was seven or eight years old.

Although our house was not noisy, I preferred to take my books and climb up my reading tree to read in peaceful solitude. My reading tree was a large oak tree that grew closer to our cabins than to the big house. This special tree branched out early at about four feet in height and made a fork that developed into two separate branches. I could easily scale the four feet and drag my beloved books up with me into the fork of the tree. The tree offered solace and silence as I traveled the world through the reading of my mother's books. Hours would slip away, as I sat absorbed completely in the stories offered by the books.

I am sure that Grandma and George knew exactly where I was, but they never bothered me while I was in my reading tree. They knew my body was in the tree but my mind was sailing through distant and mysterious lands. The reading tree allowed my imagination to soar into fictional lands and to forget the daily life on the fish camp for a short while.

I read until my legs went to sleep and my backside hurt from sitting in the tree so long. But not until hunger pangs gnawed at my stomach did I climb down from my reading tree and head toward the big house.

As I grew taller, the tree spread its forks wider, and I had a larger, more comfortable place to enjoy reading. After a while, there was a permanently worn spot in the forks, where I would sit while reading.

The reading tree was one of the things I missed when we moved away from the fish camp. There were no trees in our yard at the new place, just lots and lots of hardy Bermuda grass. Although I continued to love reading, I had to be content with sitting in a chair in our house to read. I sorely missed the peace and solitude of my comforting reading tree and hoped that someone else would enjoy its spacious branches and a good book.

Comfort And Warmth

Outgrown flour-sack blouses
Sharp, silver and black scissors
Ironed multicolored pieces of fabric stacked together
Grandma pedals the old Singer sewing machine
The Singer hums and stitches triangles, squares, diamonds and rectangles
Together in whimsical patterns
Each quilt piece is a part of our history, preserved to serve us
Each piece is a history lesson of its own
Grandma sews all the unique pieces together
And the whimsical piece together as a quilt top
Many stitches later and with batting and binding added
It becomes a quilt
Not just a quilt, though
It lives on, a comforting and warm family heirloom.

CHAPTER 2:

DADDY

WILLIAM FORD McNEW

William Ford McNew known to most as Bill or Mac, was my father and he was a kind and generous man, with his main fault being that he was an alcoholic. In the era in which he lived, alcoholism was not considered an addiction or an illness. We now know that it is both: an addiction and an illness. Unfortunately, in hardscrabble times, if you drank too much, you were a drunkard. But, alcoholism or drunkenness, did not define all that my father was. To me, he was larger than life. He was creative and not afraid to try anything new. In fact, I believe he relished doing new things, making new things and seeing new things. At age fifteen, Daddy decided that since he wasn't given a middle name, he would choose one that he liked. So, he became William Ford McNew and it stuck.

Jim Lyday wrote a book called, _The First Off The Mountain_, published in 1992, and mentioned Daddy and how he was impressed by him. He and Daddy went to the same school and they were friends. Daddy lived in the Lahusage Hotel with his parents, who were caretakers of the hotel. Mr. Lyday was surprised by Daddy's ingenious way of getting to school. Daddy would paddle his boat across Lake Lahusage, up the east branch of Little River, tie up his boat and walk the rest of the way to school. This method saved him about a mile and a half of walking the entire way to school. In his book, Mr. Lyday also mentioned that after school, as soon as he got in his boat, Daddy would reach underneath the boat seat and pull out a tennis ball. He opened the tennis ball and took out a chew (chaw) of tobacco. He wasn't allowed to chew tobacco in school, so he kept the tobacco in a tennis ball, safely tucked away in his boat.

In high school, Daddy was the quarterback for the football team. Daddy loved roaming the woods around his Mentone, Alabama, home. He hunted, fished, and did other chores like all his friends. He graduated from high school and went to work in Chattanooga, doing construction jobs. During this time he met and dated my mother for several years. My mother's oldest brother, Larry, was a machinist and worked at Combustion Engineering in Chattanooga. Uncle Larry got Daddy a job there, where he learned to weld and became a boilermaker. He and my mother were married and lived with my maternal grandparents for a while. Daddy joined the Seabees and was deployed to California, where my mother was able to join him. Later on, he would have tours in Alaska and the Philippines, so my mother returned to Chattanooga until he was home from the service. They, then, rented a small apartment and Daddy resumed his job of a boilermaker. But, it's my belief that big city life was not for my father. He longed to get away from the noise and the houses built so close to each other. On a trip with his cousin, Fred Peake, Daddy discovered that there was land for sale available near the Dead Lakes of Wewahitchka.

Though it was about four hundred miles from Chattanooga and Mentone, Daddy and Fred purchased the land and Daddy persuaded my mother to come with him on this new adventurous challenge, which would eventually become Cypress Creek Lodge.

Daddy soon made friends with the hardworking Kinard folks and when they found out that he had once worked as a butcher, he was always asked to help out on slaughtering days. Slaughtering days were planned and almost always took place on Saturdays. Many of the neighbors would come out to help the neighbor who was slaughtering his hogs. The women would bring over covered dishes that would be devoured after the hogs were slaughtered. It was sort of like a picnic atmosphere, bizarre because of the hogs being killed, but a great time for the neighbors to work together and enjoy each other's company. The actual slaughtering took place early in the mornings. Usually, three fatted hogs were chosen, shot and carried to a wooden table, where Daddy would begin the cleaning and butchering of them. He worked quickly and methodically, deftly slicing away roasts, chops, hams, ribs, and lean and fat meat to be ground into sausages. The intestines were set aside to be emptied of their contents, cleaned and washed thoroughly. The women took on this smelly job. After the contents were emptied, the intestines were turned inside out and washed again thoroughly. After the intestines were declared completely clean, they were boiled and turned into chitterlings or "chitlins" as we called them. None of the hog was wasted. The heart and the liver were cleaned and made ready to cook. The stomach was cleaned and became tripe. The hog's brains were scoured cleaned and were especially good when fried with eggs for a morning meal. Some of our neighbors also kept the hogs' hooves to turn into pickled pig's feet.

Daddy really enjoyed helping his neighbors so he didn't charge for providing his butchering services. But the neighbors always paid him in pork chops, roasts and sausages, which we kept in our small freezer until needed. Nothing ever smelled as good as hot coffee being perked and pork chops sizzling in the cast iron skillet on the stove.

The neighbors also found out that Daddy made his own delicious barbecue sauce and was a pro at barbecuing. As a result, he was asked to cook for weddings, reunions and get-togethers. On one particular social occasion, Daddy was asked to roast a fat pig. This pig was very fat and his skin made delicious cracklings which George and I were given to enjoy while Daddy tended to the pig, roasting over an open fire. Today's store-bought pig skins don't even compare to the fresh-roasted cracklings we ate when we were kids.

Truly, Daddy was a jack-of-all-trades, fearless and always ready to take on a new challenge. In the end, though, alcohol would lead to a widow-maker heart attack which claimed this talented man's life at the young age of fifty-eight.

Mac's Barbecue Sauce Recipe

2 lbs. onions, chopped	½ lb. lemons, sliced
2 stalks celery, chopped	1 lg. canned tomato paste
boxes garlic, minced	1 lg. canned tomato puree
(46 oz.) cans V-8 juice	½ lb. sugar
1 qt. stewed tomatoes	1 pt. vinegar
1 lb. green bell pepper, chopped	1 (20 oz.) Coca Cola
3 cans beer	1 (6 oz.) prepared mustard
¾ lg. bottle Worcestershire sauce	1-2 lg. bottles Catsup

1 (5 oz.) bottle soy sauce, hot pepper, black pepper, salt to taste, and 1 lb. of butter

This was Daddy's recipe in his own words. He didn't use cursive handwriting but had a particular style of printing and, thankfully, my stepmother saved the recipe. Daddy would prepare all the ingredients and put them in a huge stockpot on the electric stove, which he would set on medium heat to cook for 2 or 3 hours. He tasted the sauce several times and stirred it to keep it from sticking to the bottom of the pot. Sometimes, the heat was adjusted depending on how fast or slow the sauce cooked. The smell of the sauce permeated the air for miles, it seemed. The sauce was good by itself, but wonderful when barbecuing chickens, and the recipe makes about 2 ½ gallons of sauce. Daddy used this recipe when he made barbecued chicken for my own wedding rehearsal dinner. My mother-in-law and I made some one year and gave it as gifts. Melissa, George's daughter, made a batch one year and shared it with friends and family. Finally, to make sure this recipe lived on; I shared it in our church cookbook in 2004.

My Daddy

MY PARENTS, MR. AND MRS. WILLIAM FORD McNEW

CHAPTER 3:

MOMMA, SHIRLEY PIERCE CATE MCNEW

Shirley was my mother and because she died when my brother and I were so young, we had to rely on our relatives and friends to remind us of the things my mother did and experienced. I remember bits and pieces of her life—how she loved her family, the sun and the beach, boat rides, quilting parties, her in a beautiful pink satin bed jacket in the hospital, bringing her morphine in a tiny dark green bottle, the smell of cancer and her in a blue silk gown, lying in her coffin, suffering no more.

My uncle George, her brother, wrote lovingly of her life and I chose to share his account. He wrote that my mother was his best friend growing up and that she was a tomboy, outgoing, and had lots of friends.

Besides being his best friend, Shirley was one of the smartest people George knew. She was promoted twice while in school and although fun-loving in nature, she was very well-grounded and level-headed. Shirley saved his life one day when they were young. They were playing in an abandoned boat and Uncle George managed to cut his leg badly from his ankle to his knee. My mother knew he would die from losing blood, so she pulled him to the nearest house and knocked on the door. Neither knew the people who lived there, but it was a kind farmer and his wife. They bandaged George's leg and the farmer drove them both home. Luckily, my grandfather was home and drove George to the local doctor's office, where the doctor stitched him up. The scar from this cut remained with Uncle George all his life and he would retell this story many times over, giving thanks to my mother for saving him.

My mother developed breast cancer soon after my brother was born and although she underwent a double mastectomy, the cancer had spread viciously and she died a few weeks before her thirtieth birthday. I was five years old, and George was four. The community loved my mother and since my father did not own a suit, our neighbors pitched in to buy him one to wear to her funeral. The local funeral home was in charge of the funeral but also provided emergency ambulance service. Just before the hearse/ambulance was to carry my mother to Kinard for the service, a call came in that there was a tragic car wreck on Bristol Bridge and an ambulance was needed as soon as possible to transport the injured. My father permitted the funeral to be delayed while the ambulance took care of the injured people in the car wreck. Although it was a hot day in June and the church had no air conditioning, the congregation waited for several hours while the ambulance finished up so that they could carry my mother to the church for her funeral. That's the kind of community I grew up in. The people showed their love for my mother by remaining in that hot June church until the funeral could begin.

My father was left a widower with two young children. Several years before my mother died, my father asked his parents to move down to Florida from their mountain home in Alabama. They would take care of the fish camp and daily activities, while he worked his boilermaker job. My grandmother and grandfather sold their home to Grandma's niece and moved in to take care of things. My grandmother would take over the job of raising George and me, and my father would later marry my stepmother, A.D., who had a daughter of her own, Georgette, and together they would have two other children, my sister, Sarah, and brother, Bill.

I grew up wondering how life would have turned out had my mother lived. There are times when I miss her terribly. She left a very tangible void in my life, thanks to the wretched cancer that claimed her life. I always wanted her to see my precious children and grandchildren but now I know that she and Candy and all my other relatives and friends who are here no more are together in Heaven. And though I miss Candy greatly, I am comforted that my mother and father are keeping her company and that she is loved and happy.

CHAPTER 4:

GRANDMA-OLA GRACE FERRELL MCNEW

My grandmother was a five-foot tall giantess of a woman. It was amazing how much power and strength she had, even under the worst possible conditions. As a young girl, she had flaming red hair and this hair, I imagined, was akin to the inner fire she lit up when agitated. She didn't get angry often and was a very patient person. She told the following story which shows her perseverance and dignity. When she was around seven or eight years old, as she was getting ready for school, she discovered that she had no clean panties to wear. No bloomers either! She told her mother about the dilemma, but great-grandmother Ferrell simply brushed Grandma's hair and plaited it into two long shiny braids tied with white ribbons. She made sure Grandma's gingham dress looked neat and tidy and sent her to school sans pants! It was a windy day and although Grandma had on a long dress, the wind caught her billowing skirt, causing it to fly toward her head. Grandma tripped and fell, and the skirt fell over her head, exposing her bare bottom to all. I'm sure she was humiliated because she said all the boys laughed at her. But she got up, yanked her skirt down, stomped the dust off her button-up boots, and continued to play on the playground until the recess bell called everyone inside. After that, Grandma swears she never wore panties or bloomers again. When pantyhose were invented, Grandma found out that she liked them and wore them to keep her legs warm.

Grandma didn't like to be around people who cussed and she certainly did not allow us to be around them. Her usual special words were "Heavens to Betsy," "Lord have mercy" or "Lordie Mercy", "I swan" or "I swear." However, she did have three words she considered to be innocent—ass, piss and shit. Now, when Grandma said "shit," with her Alabama accent, it came as two syllables—she-ut. Ass was paired with jack, dumb or shit. If a person was constantly in trouble, he was a jackass. If a person seemed as if he had just fallen off the latest passing turnip truck, he was considered a dumbass. And, bless his heart, if he was both mischievous and slow, well, he was just a she-ut ass! Piss could be a noun, verb, adverb or adjective. "I am so pissed off! I just found another piss ant bed close to the garden!"

MR. AND MRS. WILEY FRED MCNEW

GRANDMA AND DAD AT THE LAKE LAHUSAGE HOTEL

At one point in her life, Grandma taught school in Alabama. I don't know how this came about but she mentioned it many times. After she and my grandfather married, they became caretakers of the Lake Lahusage Hotel and this is recorded in Jim Lyday's book and also several newspaper accounts of the day. She told the story of how a young black man, Mr. Jolly, would bring his dress slacks to her each week so that she could press them for him to wear on Sunday morning to church. The hotel was a three-story affair mostly, but not quite completed, and had many beds. Mr. Jolly knew this and asked Grandma to place his slacks underneath one of the hotel's many mattresses and leave them so that they would be freshly pressed for Sunday. He also used some of the lard Grandma gave him for different things, one being to put on his hair.

Another favorite story of Grandma's was of a lean time during her marriage when they were living at their home, Dad's blacksmithy work was down and he chose to go hunting one afternoon, in the hope that he would bring home fresh meat for supper. Turkeys, deer, rabbits and squirrels lived in the woods nearby, so Dad hoped he would bag at least one of these. Grandma was home, making do with what she had when she happened to look out their front window. There, in a pine tree only a few yards away, sat a huge wild turkey. Instinctively, Grandma grabbed a gun and hurried out to shoot the turkey. Admittedly, she was not a marksman, but she was determined to try. She aimed and squeezed the trigger. The large turkey fell from the pine and another fell from another pine. One turkey had been roosting directly behind the other. By the time Dad got home with three squirrels, Grandma had two clean turkeys ready to be roasted, lying on the kitchen table. Dad was flummoxed and had trouble believing Grandma's story. I did, too, but who am I to argue with a woman like her?!

Grandma, seemingly, was born with a tenacious spirit. When she was five or six years old, she convinced her mother to give her a dip of her snuff. Great Grandmother Ferrell thought that the taste of the snuff would sicken my grandmother and she wouldn't ask again for a dip. Great Grandmother was wrong! Grandma loved snuff and continued to dip for most of the rest of her life. Whenever we would fuss at her for dipping, she would say, "Oh, y'all hush! I have been dipping since I was five years old and I'm not about to stop now!" And, she didn't! Her favorite brand of snuff was Top's Sweet Snuff and if, Heaven forbid, she ran out of snuff, there was Hell to pay. Her flaming red hair had long since turned snowy white, but it seemed to sizzle as she searched high and low for her snuff. Instead of telling us that she was out, she would look here and there, rattling pots and pans and mumbling to herself. When it finally dawned on us that she was looking for her snuff, we would ask if she was out of snuff. "No," she'd snap. "I just can't find it!" When we would return from the store with her Top's, she would take a dip and her demeanor would mellow out considerably. To tease and aggravate her, sometimes my husband, Jerry, would hide her snuff. After she had searched and grumbled for a while, Jerry would produce the snuff and Grandma would take it mumbling something that sounded like, "She-ut! I should have known he hid it!"

Grandma was very good to George and me. But, every so often, she would say, "Marilyn, go get me a keen withe!" This usually meant George was in trouble and a withe was his punishment. Withes are slender limbs from a tree and Grandma knew just how to make these pop our skinny legs and wrap around them so that the maximum punishment was meted out. At the age of sixty, Grandma took on the job of raising George and me, and she put all her energy into this daunting task. God was watching over George and me when he sent Grandma to us, and we are eternally grateful for this.

I wish I could list all of the things Grandma taught us as we were growing up, but that's impossible. Grandma relied heavily on her Bible and Ben Franklin's Almanac, as well as her own good sense. Here are a few of her gems, in no certain order:

1. Do unto others as you would have them do unto you.
2. Cleanliness is next to Godliness.
3. Honesty is the best policy.
4. Clean your plate. Folks in China don't have enough to eat.
5. Stand up straight.
6. A penny saved is a penny earned.
7. Don't put all your eggs in one basket.
8. Pretty is as pretty does.
9. Anything worth doing is worth doing well.
10. Finish what you started.
11. Spare the rod. Spoil the child.
12. Make do.
13. Share your wealth with others.

14. Obey your elders

15. Always say "please", "thank you" ,"Yes Ma'am" ,"No Ma'am", "Yes Sir", "No Sir".

16. "Three sheets to the wind," had nothing to do with laundry. It meant you were sloppy drunk.

The one most important thing Grandma taught us was to "Bloom where you are planted." Her life was an epitome of this motto. I still picture her, apron on, a dip of snuff in her lip, white hair piled in a bun on her head and smiling a satisfied smile. Thank you, Grandma!

More Grandma Stories

GRANDMA'S TEA CAKES

Grandma had a sweet tooth, and as a rule, for breakfast, she would always have big cathead biscuits, which she would butter for you. There would be grape jelly or fig preserves to eat with the buttered biscuits. She also had a recipe for a plain cake or tea cakes, as she called them. If we were having company, she'd usually whip up the cake, but for us, she would make tea cakes—the recipe was exactly the same. You simply poured the mixture in a cake pan if you were making a cake or dropped the mixture by the spoonful if you were baking cookies. Sometimes, as with the cake, she would put homemade confectioner's sugar icing on the cookies. Otherwise, the cookies were plain, chewy and moist. She always made the cookies large, about the size of a Maxwell House Coffee can lid. As soon as Grandma pulled the aromatic cookie sheet from the oven, George and I would each take a cookie and enjoy it with a glass of milk. Here is Grandma's recipe:

Grandma's 1-2-3-4 Cake or Tea Cake Recipe

Ingredients:

1 cup shortening

2 cups sugar

3 cups flour

4 large eggs

Vanilla (or your choice of extract)

Directions: Heat oven to 350 degrees. Grease and flour cake pan or pans. Mix all ingredients well and pour them into the readied pans. Bake for approximately fifty minutes or until golden brown. The cake is a really chewy pound cake and turns out pretty. Sometimes, if Grandma thought the mixture was too thick, she'd add milk to soften it. The cookies turn out soft and chewy, also. Many times, Grandma would make confectioner's sugar icing for the cake, but most of the time, we ate the cake without the added icing and it was delicious.

A NEW BLANK, BLANK, BLANK, BLANK

When Grandma and Dad were married, they lived so far away from Grandma's parents that she had to write to her mother about anything new that happened in their lives. Imagine her surprise and delight when my great-grandmother got a letter from her daughter saying that she and Dad had a "new __ __ __ __". Great-grandmother Ferrell thought the four blanks meant "BABY." She must have been really disappointed when Grandma and Dad drove up in their new Ford! I'm sure she was very happy for them though, since very few neighbors had cars back then.

COMPANY MEAL

Living as far out "in the woods" as we did, could be lonely at times. There were always chores to be done and we constantly could stay busy doing them, but many times we longed for "company" to visit. Both my mother's family from Tennessee and my father's family from Alabama, Georgia, Tennessee, and Mississippi, visited as often as possible. When they did get to visit, it was always a treat for us.

Grandma had this saying, "My nose itches. Company's a coming!" Her nose wasn't always right, but when it was, we thoroughly enjoyed our company's visits. It was a huge deal, especially for Grandma, who would busy herself getting the shared meal together.

We ate breakfast, dinner, and supper, in that order. Dinner was our noon meal. (I don't remember the word "lunch" ever being used to describe our noon meal.) To get dinner started, Grandma would go out into the yard and catch one of our free-range chickens. We had about twenty or so chickens, some of which were Guinea hens, a strange-looking breed of chicken with black and white spots and oddly shaped beaks and heads. Grandma with her short skinny legs was incredibly quick at cornering an unsuspecting chicken and wringing its neck in one swift motion. The chicken didn't even have time to squawk! After chopping the chicken's head off, Grandma would dunk the body into a tub of boiling hot water. The smell of wet chicken feathers was not pleasant, but we would all defeather the poor creature as soon as possible. Then, Grandma would light a rolled-up section of a newspaper with a match and begin to singe the fuzz and lingering feathers off. She would hold the chicken and let the flames from the newspaper lick away any errant feathers or fuzz and then, once again, dunk the chicken in the tub of hot water. Inside the house, the cleaning would resume, as Grandma split the chicken open and removed the innards. The heart, and liver and gizzard were washed and frozen to be eaten at a later time. Grandma cut the rest of the chicken up into frying sections and put these into the refrigerator. We would go out into the garden to gather fresh vegetables to complete the dinner meal. We grew field peas, corn, okra, tomatoes, greens, pota- toes, onions, watermelon, butterbeans, and pole beans, depending on what season of the year it was, and what the Ben Franklin's Almanac recommended. While the vegetables cooked, Grandma fried the chicken in a big iron skillet, made biscuits or cornbread, and managed to get everything ready in time for dinner. If she had time, she would whip up one of her 1-2-3-4 cakes. If not, a jar of homemade fig preserves or blackberry jelly would be placed on the table to be eaten with biscuits for des- sert. Other times, for dessert after dinner, we would gather on the back porch and make homemade vanilla ice cream, making sure everyone had a chance to crank the old wooden ice cream bucket. Company meals were never rushed but enjoyed and savored as friendly conversation flowed back and forth, as everyone caught up on the news from the visiting relatives.

RECIPE FOR DISASTER

Grandma had a tried and true cake recipe which she called her "1-2-3-4 Cake Recipe" previously mentioned. Grandma favored almond extract, which she purchased from the Burkett's Watkins' Peddler Truck. Grandma used her cake recipe to make what she called "tea cakes," small flat cookies with extra sugar sprinkled on top. Her cakes and cookies were rarely frosted since frosting required powdered sugar, which unlike the first four items; we did not normally have on hand. But, on occasions when we knew "company was coming," Grandma would whip up some fantastic frost- ing. On one particular day when she knew we were having relatives drive down from Alabama, Grandma decided to fancy up her usual cake with some chocolate icing. First, she creamed butter, milk, powdered sugar, and cocoa, and the icing was looking simply scrumptious. All that was needed was for two teaspoons of vanilla extract to be added to the batter. Reaching behind her, Grandma picked up a tall brown Watkin's bottle and measured out two level teaspoons and added them to the icing mix. Immediately, a strong odor permeated the air, not a vanilla or chocolate smell, but a sick-room smell. Upon inspecting the bottle, Grandma learned she had flavored the frosting with Watkins' Reliable Liniment! "She-ut!" was all she said, as the bottle of vanilla sat on the shelf, unopened. Never the quitter (Grandma put the Grrr in Grit), Grandma disposed of the tainted icing and started over again from scratch. The Watkins' Vanilla Extract bottle and the Watkins' Reliable Liniment bottle remained side by side on our open shelf, along with the other Watkins' products. But Grandma never whipped up another batch of icing without checking the labels on the bottles of extracts!

"JUST OUR SON"

One of the highlights of living at the fish camp was the monthly visit from the Watkins' peddlers, the Burketts from Port St. Joe. Mr. and Mrs. Burkett were friendly outgoing people and getting to know them was a pleasure. Although he didn't try to "hard sell" us on his products, Mr. Burkett was a true believer in his Watkins' products and was more than happy to show us the new stuff. Watkins products were invented by Joseph Ray Watkins, an American entrepreneur, who made homemade extracts, liniments, and salves. Mr. Watkins offered a money-back guarantee for his products and is credited as the founder of the direct sales industry. Watkins products are still available today, however, the bottles and signage on the products have been modernized. What I remember is seeing dozens and dozens of amber brown bottles lined up on the inside of the Burketts' covered pickup truck. The Burketts would drive up in their old pick-up truck, and George and I would run out to see what treasures they had brought to sell. Grandma became good friends with Mr. and Mrs. Burkett and always bought items from their loaded truck. The Burkett family came inland to stay at our fish camp on several occasions when a hurricane threatened the Gulf. We were all invited to their home, which was on Port St. Joe Beach to go "crabbing," another new adventure for me. One spring morning, Grandma read in the paper that a gas station owner had been shot and killed during an armed robbery. The man's last name was Burkett and that made Grandma wonder if he had been related to the Burketts we knew. It seemed quite a long stretch of time before we heard the old truck rumble up our driveway, carrying the Watkins' products. As usual, we ran out to greet them. Grandma hurried along behind us and after telling the Burketts how glad we were to see them, asked, "Was that Burkett man killed in St. Joe any kin to y'all?" Mrs. Burkett sadly and softly replied, "Just our son, Mrs. Mac." It was a sad day for all. Their son's killer was eventually caught, tried and convicted, giving some peace of mind to the grieving Burkett family. If my memory serves me accurately, Mr. and Mrs. Burkett continued to sell Watkins products until Mr. Burkett's health began to fail. After their son's death, it seemed that they sort of lost their joy of being peddlers. Grief is a real joy robber.

THE BUSINESS OF THE BIRDS AND BEES

Grandma never gave me "the talk," and I suppose it was a hard subject for my father to discuss with me, so as a result, I didn't find out where babies came from until I was in the second grade. At recess one day, a classmate sat down beside me on the playground. I didn't care a lot for this classmate because he was constantly in trouble for goading the other boys into a fight. He usually got the better of his opponent, but then, he would be chastised by the teachers for fighting. This particular day, for no apparent reason, he plopped down next to me on the pine straw covered playground and said, "See that fat lady over there?" He was referring to Nadine Stone, whose family owned the general store across the street from the school. It wasn't unusual for Mrs. Stone to visit since her children attended school there. But, I hadn't noticed that she was truly getting pudgy, especially around her midsection. "I see her," I said. "She's gonna have a baby," he replied. "How do YOU know?" I questioned him. "See her belly? The baby's in there!" he smugly explained. "Is not," I yelled. "Is too," he yelled back, grinning widely. We argued back and forth for a while and I finally ended the argument by jumping up and yelling, "I'm gonna ask my grandma," before running off toward the school building. Later, when school was over for the day, I couldn't wait to jump off the bus and race up the hill to find Grandma. She was at the stove, stirring a pot of pinto beans, when I burst in saying, "A boy at school told me Mrs. Stone has a baby in her stomach. Is that true?" Not perturbed in the least, Grandma simply said, "Wait and see!" What?! Not the answer I was looking for! About three months later, Mrs. Stone did have a baby and I was enlightened about pregnancy and childbirth!

THE CANDY MAN MYSTERY

George and I must have been two of the luckiest children in our rural area because we had our very own candy man. He was one of our fish camp guests, a kindhearted candy salesman from Georgia, named Bill Boynton. Mr. Boynton would drive down from Georgia, in his big Cadillac, rent a cabin and fish all weekend. Before he checked into his cabin, he would have George and me come out to his car. As he unlocked the trunk and began to raise it up, we could see boxes and boxes of candy that he had brought for us. It was candy that he had had to pull off the shelf because it was out of date, but we never noticed any difference in taste and thoroughly enjoyed all the sweet snacks. My favorites were the candy cigarettes and the tiny wax bottles of sugary water. Because there was so much candy, we were allowed to take some to school and share it with our friends. We thought Mr. Boynton was the richest man in the world, and to us, he was "The Candy Man."In later years, when our cabins were no longer being rented out, Mr. Boynton would still make the trip down but he would stay in a neighboring fish camp. He always came over to see us and he always brought us candy. One summer, while Mr. Boynton was fishing, thieves broke into the cabin where he was staying and ransacked the place. They took his big leather suitcase, which Mr. Boynton had left opened, and got away, without ever being caught. The local sheriff was called and everyone thought it was an "inside job" but no one was ever charged or caught. Mr. Boynton stopped by to tell us what had happened. We were shocked and angered that someone had stolen from our beloved candy man. Mr. Boynton told us that his only regret was that inside the suitcase, he had left his gold cufflinks and he really hated to lose them.

About a year later, Daddy decided that we needed to clean out the swampy area next to the highway because it was overgrown and moccasins flourished in places like that. The highway had very steep ditches and our driveway began where the ditches connected on either side. It was nasty work, but necessary, and each of us had a job. Daddy had a large machete with which he chopped down large bushes and palmetto ferns. Our main assignment was to spread out and pull up or dig up as much of the scruffy underbrush as possible and to watch for snakes that could be hiding beneath. Just as I bent down to pull up a weird stinky plant (which I later learned was a Venus Flytrap), I heard Grandma yell out that she had found something. She had been pulling weeds near the highway's deep ditch. We all gathered around as she pulled out a large leather suitcase from the dense underbrush.

Although covered with ferns and some of the swampy mud, the suitcase appeared none the worse for wear. As Grandma unhooked the suitcase's latches, Mr. Boynton's clothes and papers began to appear. Apparently, the thieves had taken the suitcase, stolen Mr. Boynton's wallet, which contained about two hundred dollars in cash, and then thrown the suitcase over into the ditch as they drove away. Remembering that Mr. Boynton had mentioned his lost cufflinks; Grandma dug into one of the pockets in the suitcase and pulled out a small black jewelry box. Inside, in perfect condition, were the gold cufflinks.

Daddy drove to a neighbor's house to borrow their phone and called Mr. Boynton. That weekend, Mr. Boynton drove down in his big Cadillac and insisted on paying Grandma for finding his missing cufflinks. I don't think he knew how stubborn and strong-willed my grandmother could be. She simply refused to take money from a good friend.

Mr. Boynton remained a true friend. Years later, when my father passed away, he drove down from Georgia, once again in another big Cadillac. He wanted to drive my grandmother to my father's funeral. At that time, we were not living at the fishcamp and the land between my grandmother's house and my father's house had been plowed up to be planted with vegetables. Mr. Boynton visited my stepmother and then started to Grandma's. He didn't figure that the soft black mud would be a problem, but it was, and soon his Cadillac was up to its wheel covers in the mud. He rode with us to Daddy's funeral.

After the funeral, one of our kind neighbors came over in his pick-up truck and managed to pull Mr. Boynton's Cadillac out of the mud. He headed back to his home in Georgia and that was the last time I saw him. But, Mr. Boynton, a.k.a. "The Candy Man" remains, literally, a sweet childhood memory for me.

THE LOST PEARLS

Once a Georgia relative got married, and she and her new husband chose our fish camp as their honeymoon spot. It was the perfect place to have privacy for the new-lyweds. They only stayed for the weekend since they both had jobs to return to in Georgia. Grandma fixed a big country breakfast for them before their early departure, and then she walked down to the cabin they had occupied to clean it. Lying under-neath the bed, she found a string of pearls that the relative had forgotten or misplaced.

Grandma put the string of pearls in her apron pocket and finished cleaning the cabin. When she got back to the "big house" as we called it, she dropped the pearls into my mother's china teapot. Near dusk, the newlyweds came back to our house, and the relative was in a frantic state. "Please tell me you found my pearl necklace, Aunt Ola!" she cried. "Why, course I did, Honey. It was under y'all's bed," Grandma replied. I remember the newlyweds sheepishly blushing but being happily relieved. Grandma then retrieved the necklace from the teapot and gave it to the bride. As it turns out, the necklace was a wedding gift for the bride from her new husband and it was quite valuable. The new bride only remembered the necklace after they had driven halfway back to their home in Georgia.

TURTLE-WHITE MEAT FROM THE CREEK

Aunt Frances, my mother's sister, loved coming down from Chattanooga to visit us. She and Granddaddy Cate would leave their home in Chattanooga early in the morning for the roughly ten-hour drive to Kinard. It was a joyous family time when, at last, they would arrive shortly before sunset. Grandma had been cooking most of the day, and of course, had prepared an excellent dinner. The menu for this partic-ular day was smother-fried turtle, coleslaw, fresh onions, tomatoes, cucumbers, new potatoes boiled with pole beans, and biscuits. Unlike my mother, Aunt Frances wasn't too keen on trying new foods and had always said she loved us dearly, but she would never eat frog legs or turtle. Grandma knew this and hoped Aunt Frances would not be offended since she had cooked turtle. The thing was, she purposely didn't tell Aunt Frances that the meat frying in the large cast-iron skillet was turtle. I must have been around three or four years old and would not have remembered this story if it had not been told over and over again by my aunt and uncle. As the story goes, everyone was enjoying the meal when Aunt Frances remarked, "Mrs. Mac, this is the best chicken I have ever tasted!" At that moment, I said, "Aunt Frances, dat's not chicken! Dat's tuttle!" Grandma shot me an evil look and time froze.

Everyone looked at my aunt. She sat there for a minute and then burst out laughing! "Well, Mrs. Mac, you got me good and from now on, I would be happy to eat 'tuttle!' True to her word, she did eat turtle after that and managed to develop a liking for frog legs. However, none of us liked to watch the frog legs cooking because they move as they are dropped into the frying pan!

GRAPES, FIGS, AND GOOD NEIGHBORS

There were two large grape vines on our property, which afforded us wonderful snacks and tasty jams and jellies. The two grape vines produced different grapes,-one had large purplish-pink grapes and the other had tiny pinkish cluster grapes. Both varieties were delicious. Anyone who visited was urged to pick their fill of the grapes. Grandma became friends with Rainey, a jovial African American woman who lived in a small house on the road to Chipola Park Inn. Rainey worked for the Inn and kept her children and her tiny house neat and tidy. She raised a garden, had free-range chickens and a large fig tree. She and Grandma got together and Rainey came over and picked grapes. Grandma then went to Rainey's home and picked figs, which she turned into fig preserves. There were very few African Americans who lived in the area at the time, and at times prejudice and racism would rear their ugly heads. But, George and I were not raised to be prejudiced and Rainey was not only a friend, but she was also a valued and good neighbor.

YES, LIGHTNING DOES STRIKE TWICE!

Grandma was not afraid of much but there was one thing that always bothered her and that was lightning. Now, all of us hated the sudden thunderstorms that sprang up and probably should have been more aware of the destruction they could and did cause. But what really aggravated us most was that the electricity would go off as quickly as the storm came up. Grandma would disappear into the bedroom and sit on the bed, just sit and think and probably pray. When the storm would pass, Grandma would be herself again and go about her regular routine. She had good reason to be afraid of lightning since it did strike our house twice. Each time, we would hear a deafening bomb-like noise, and then it would be over. The first strike caused no damage. The second one caused the side of the roof to catch fire and singed the asphalt shingles. There was not a lot of damage, but it was scary, and Grandma never got over her fear of lightning.

HARDSCRABBLE DAYS

Many times Daddy would have to travel in his job as a boilermaker to what seemed like exotic places to me as a child growing up in northwest Florida. He would go as far away sometimes as Mobile, Alabama, or Pascagoula, Mississippi. We did not own a phone or a car, so while he was gone, Grandma had some hardscrabble days if she ran out of staples to make meals. As a rule, she usually had staples of flour, cooking oil, coffee, cornmeal and sugar. Always we had the garden and the hens provided eggs or surrendered their bodies for meals. But, there were other necessities we'd run out of and Grandma found ways to "make do." Once, I remember Daddy had been gone for a long while and supplies were running short. For lunch (dinner, as we called it), Grandma, George, and I ate fried "fatback" with biscuits, and it was good. However, I was glad to see Daddy's car pull up that afternoon and realize that we would indeed be able to go to the grocery store. We had wonderful neighbors, although they were not next-door neighbors as we think of today. To visit our nearest neighbors, we had to walk "a piece" but each of these neighbors would have helped us out if they had known we were in need of anything. They didn't know because Grandma didn't let them know. Part of this was Grandma's pride, but most of it came from her hillbilly roots which served her well. She had been raised to live off the land and that is what she knew how to do. She used the term "make do" many times in my childhood, and I find myself using it while staring at a well-stocked pantry, but not wanting to use any of the items to make a meal from. Grandma would have whipped up a meal fit for a king from my pantry, but somehow, the taste of the hardscrabble meal of fatback and biscuits seems to me to have been one of her finest.

CHAPTER 5:

FAMILY AND FRIENDS

GRANDDADDY CATE

George Oscar Cate, Sr. was my mother's father. I never had the privilege of meeting my grandmother, Anne Palmer Cate, because she passed away in 1946, before I was born in 1949. My grandfather, though, was quite a character, and an unforgettable memory of my growing up years. He lived in Chattanooga, Tennessee, with his daughter, my aunt Frances. Aunt Frances had moved back home after her mother became sick so that she could become my grandmother's caregiver.

She and Granddaddy Cate would, when financially possible, drive the four hundred miles to the fish camp to visit us. What a treat that was! When my mother was still alive, their visit always called for a trip to Mexico Beach. As I remember it, we'd all pile into Granddaddy's sedan, having packed sandwiches and a watermelon for lunch, and head toward the white sands of the beach. Daddy would dig deep into the crystal sands and bury the watermelon so that it would be crisp and cold by lunchtime. Then, after settling our things down on the hot sand, we'd spend the rest of the morning splashing away in the gulf's waters. Granddaddy was a quiet man, but he had a commanding presence. He usually got wet, then sat on the seashore and watched as the rest of us played. Grandma, who never wore slacks a day in her life, had a navy blue skirted swimsuit. The suit had white polka dots on it and fitted Grandma nicely. It was the only time in my life that I saw Grandma wear anything except her usual dress and apron. At that time, Mexico Beach had outdoor showers and picnic tables. After a shower and a good lunch, we would head back home. Granddaddy would have his coffee and talk with my parents and Aunt Frances while Grandma started supper. Grandma remarked that "Mister George sure likes his coffee but he sure makes a noise stirring it up." My grandfather had a habit of swirling a spoon around and around in his cup, creating a tinkling sound by doing so. After dinner, Granddaddy would usually leave the big house and walk down to one of our cabins that he and Aunt Frances shared and go to bed. My mother and Aunt Frances would catch up on each other's news, while George and I were put to bed. The next morning Daddy and Granddaddy would go fishing in the Dead Lakes and Aunt

Frances, Momma, George and I traveled to Panama City, to shop. I loved the times that they got to spend with us, even though they usually only stayed for four days.

Her siblings declared that Momma was Granddaddy's favorite child and they were not jealous of this because they knew they were also loved. They also believed that Granddaddy grieved silently after my mother passed away and, eventually, this grieving led to his death of a massive heart attack when I was about eleven years old. It was a sad time, made more so by the suddenness of it all.

Granddaddy had been through the Great Depression and lost a lot of money, but although he had many jobs in his lifetime, he was really shrewd at the real estate business. Uncle George described him as "tight fisted" with his money. At one time, he owned a grocery store, but when I when I was born, he was the owner of Central Dry Cleaners in Chattanooga.

For years, he and Aunt Frances lived on Kyle Street in Chattanooga. The house was two-storied and there were thirty-two steps from the street up to the house. At times, the second story was rented out because they lived in the upper story and had plenty of space. It was a nice home, much more refined than ours, but at that time, Chattanooga was a dirty city and any clothes hung on the line to dry would gather a layer of smoky dust on them and had to be vigorously shaken before ironing. Since then, the people of Chattanooga have cleaned up their beautiful city and have been applauded for doing so.

After my mother passed away, the state of Tennessee paid my grandfather a good sum of money because they were coming through with a freeway, and Granddaddy's home was to be torn down. Granddaddy took the money and divided it among his children, splitting what would have been my mother's share between George and me. The money was put into a trust, which George and I was allowed to access when we turned twenty-one. When I turned twenty-one, George and I drove up to Chattanooga and claimed my miraculous inheritance. I used it as a down payment on a car, since I was at that time, going to the University of West Florida, and I did not have transportation. Many years later, my aunt Clara called me saying that we had some more money due us. It seems that somehow another real estate transaction was made by Granddaddy and our share was banked and forgotten about. A clerk in the city court noticed that a 'Cate' was mentioned in the "unclaimed monies" section and remembered that Aunt Clara, her friend, was a Cate! She called Aunt Clara and Aunt Clara set the whole thing in motion for George and I to once again inherit what had grown to become a sizeable amount over the years. I think "tight-fisted" George knew all along that this would happen. He was a wonderful grandfather.

MY MATERNAL GRANDPARENTS, GEORGE AND ANNE CATE

SHIRLEY GRACE

Shirley Grace Lindsay Kittle is my first cousin, the middle child of my father's sister, Nellie. She was a huge part of my growing up years, even though she was married with five children and lived in Ocean Springs, Mississippi. Shirley Grace tried to visit us each year and we thoroughly enjoyed her visits. Grandma said, "That Shirley Grace can talk the horns off a billy goat!" which was and is true and one of the reasons why we love her. Shirley Grace was named after my mother, Shirley, and my grandmother, Ola Grace. Shirley Grace loved Grandma and the feeling was mutual. And now, even though I don't talk with her often, Shirley Grace is on Facebook daily, so we keep in touch via the internet.

After her fifth child was born, Shirley had a nervous breakdown, or what today would probably be diagnosed as post-partum depression. But, in those days, PPD was not a recognizable illness, so Shirley's doctor called it a nervous breakdown and recommended she get away from her family for a while to rest. Her husband, Frank, got his mother to watch their children and brought Shirley Grace to stay with us. Of course, we were delighted and Shirley seemed happy. Being the oldest, I never had a big sister, but Shirley came close to filling the void. She kept us entertained with her stories and never seemed to be depressed. Later, I would ask her how she remained so positive and she replied, "You can hide a lot behind a smile!" Frank's mother found handling the Kittle clan to be more than she bargained for, and Frank came back to pick Shirley up after two short weeks. We missed her terribly but were glad that the two weeks seemed to give Shirley the respite that she needed.

One Christmas season, Shirley Grace drove over to spend the holiday with us. I don't remember her husband coming with her but she brought all her children. George and I were not taught about hanging stockings but Shirley Grace's children were, so that night, Shirley Grace borrowed some of my father's long work socks, and George and I helped her fill the socks with oranges and nuts. The final treats were those sticky hard candies, which in those days were unwrapped so that they stuck to the inside of the socks. That Christmas, Uncle Alfred, Shirley Grace's father, had bought pajamas for all the kids and they wore them to bed on Christmas Eve. Their only toy was Hasbro's Mouse Trap game which Shirley Grace put under the pine tree we had sparsely decorated with ancient Christmas ornaments and recycled tinsel. On Christmas morning, the Kittle kids woke up and were thrilled with the stockings, even the sticky candy parts and loved the new game. George and I were older than the cousins, but not by many years and we also loved playing the new game with them. It must have been a mild Christmas day because we played outside after Mouse Trapping for quite a while. George and I took turns pulling Kelly Marie, and Quintin J in our wagon. We hit some bumpy grasses and Kelly fell out. I was horrified that we had hurt her but she got up laughing. I was relieved!

Shirley has always had a sense of humor and her giggles are contagious! Not being able to afford Christmas cards one year, she sent us a handmade card, complete with her own drawing of her family of five and captioned it: "Merry Christmas from Shirley, Frank, and the five little pots!"

Sadly, Frank has passed away, but Shirley and her five little pots are thriving and are spread out over the United States with their families: Frank Jr. is retired from being the Coliseum's Zamboni engineer and lives in Ocean Springs, Mississippi; Angelyn lives in Bastrop, Texas, and is the office manager of a veterinarian's office; Cecelia is the Goodwill Industries executive secretary in Oklahoma City, Oklahoma; Kelly is an auditor living in Huntsville, Alabama; and Quentin has his own architectural firm in Pittsburg, Pennsylvania.

Shirley also lives in Huntsville and continues to amaze me with her stories of growing up in Chattanooga, Tennessee. She is a special cousin!

AUNT NELLIE

Something wakes me and I try to shake off the confines of sleep. There it is again—the noise that has yanked me from a deep, deep sleep. I sit up and try to rid my fuzzy brain of the last lingering fingers of sleep. Again I hear the noise; and this time, I recognize what it is. The sharp calls of a freight train, sounding hauntingly lonesome and decidedly near, causes me to recall the events of yesterday. I look at my brother, George, sleeping soundly, on the soft couch where we had both dozed off, late last night. I remember now what had happened and the long bus ride we had taken to get us to see our Aunt Nellie, Grandma's only daughter, who lived with her family in Chattanooga, Tennessee. Aunt Nellie was dying of wicked breast cancer and Grandma had wanted to visit and help out as much as she could. Daddy had taken us to the bus depot in Blountstown and from there we traveled the four hundred miles to Chattanooga. It had been quite an experience for us since we had never been on a Trailways bus before. We had taken several changes of clothes in a pillowcase and Grandma carried what little money she had in a knotted handkerchief. She had ridden on the outside of the bench, while George and I sat next to the window. Sometime after darkness arrived, we all fell asleep. Grandma dropped the handkerchief. A kind gentleman woke her up and returned the handkerchief. The bus parked at the Chattanooga station and Grandma got us into a cab, another new thing for us! It was very late when we arrived at Aunt Nellie's house, so we went into her parlor (no one locked doors back then), and fell asleep on the couch.

The train noise neared and a good smell was wafting in from somewhere in the house. Grandma was nowhere to be found so George, now fully awake, and I jumped off the couch and followed the smell into the kitchen. Grandma had fried bacon and eggs and made her cathead biscuits for breakfast, and I was fascinated by what my cousin Alfreda was doing. Deftly using her knife and fork, Alfreda was meticulously shredding her soft fried eggs into tiny pieces and allowing the yellow yolk to ooze out and fill her plate. Aunt Nellie's three daughters Nell, Shirley Grace, and Alfreda, were all older than George and me, but we would have something in common soon, that would bind us tragically together forever—Aunt Nellie, like our mother, would lose her battle with breast cancer, and her three daughters would be motherless. My grandmother must have been so torn, what with caring for us, and wanting to be with her only daughter, who truly needed her, too. Grandma stoically never complained but went about taking care of Aunt Nellie, making meals, and keeping house. I remember we stayed only a week, then Uncle Alfred took us to the bus station for the trip back home. We must have met our aunt while we were there, but I can't remember seeing her. I never saw Grandma shed a tear, but I know her heart was breaking when the bus headed toward Florida. She would never see her daughter alive again. I feel so blessed that I had fifteen months with my daughter as she courageously fought the cancer beast. I was there for her final goodbye and I feel badly that my grandmother never had that privilege with her daughter.

AUNT NELLIE AND UNCLE ALFRED AND THEIR GIRLS

THE FORTNER FAMILY

The Fortner family lived down the road from us and was a huge influence on my life. Leroy and Bernice Fortner had four children when we first got to know them. Later in life, Mrs. Bernice gave birth to another little girl but we never got to know her because by then the Fortners had moved to Wewahitchka and we didn't see them often. We did know Charles (Scootsie), Willie Joe (Dude), Sue (Soo Soo), and Faye (Faysie). Charles was a year older than me, Willie Joe and George were the same age, and the two girls were years younger.

"Miss Bernice," as we called her, drove our school bus and Sue and Faye would ride along her route with her since they were not old enough to go to school. Sue talked plainly since she was older, but Faye had trouble pronouncing some words. Cheryl and I loved playing with these two little girls as we rode along to school and were delighted when Faye first began calling us by name. I was "Mullen" and Cheryl became "Sull."

We were saddened when the Fortner family sold their home and moved to Wewahitchka, but every Saturday they would drive to Blountstown to buy groceries, and Sue and Faye would stay with us while they shopped. During the summer months, I would go home with the girls and spend a few days until Miss Bernice drove me back home. Sue, Faye and I would walk to the lake in town and swim, and play on the playground. If I had any money, I would buy us some snacks for a picnic. At night, Scootsie and Dude would go outside under the street lights and play ball with the neighbor boys.

Years later, when Grandma passed away, Sue and her mother came to the funeral. Sue had grown into a beautiful young lady and worked at the Wewahitchka Pharmacy. She thanked me profusely for spending time with her and Faye during their childhood, but I assured her that I enjoyed being with them as much as they enjoyed being with me. Every time I think about "Mullen and Sull," it brings a smile to my face!

*Charles, "Scootsie" Fortner passed away in June of 2018, another part of my childhood gone.

In May of 2019, I once again would get the chance to see Sue and her mother in Blountstown. Sue is married and has children and grandchildren and Mrs. Bernice looks almost the same, maybe with a few more well-deserved grey hairs! At this meeting, several other old friends came—Jean Hill Flowers, Winifred Waldroff, and Minnie and Rodney Johnson. Odeen Flowers and Tommy Skipper dropped by, too. What a wonderful blessing to get to see these old friends who helped shape my life and were still willing to give up a day to meet with me!

THE HARBESON FAMILY

Mr. and Mrs. Harbeson lived across the creek from us on a fish camp of their own. Their fish camp was similar to ours, with three small cabins but, unlike ours, theirs had a dock which extended out into the dark creek water, with wooden boats tied to poles rising above the dock.

My mother became fast friends with the Harbeson's daughter, Marie McClellan. Marie was married and lived in Blountstown, but came down often to her parents' home. Marie and her husband had three sons and the two older ones, Jerry and Sammy, would later be the only guests at my birthday party when I turned two. Sammy and I graduated from high school the same year and he married one of my good friends. Sadly, Sammy passed away several years ago.

My mother and father took me in one of our boats and paddled over to the Harbesons to show me off when I was two weeks old. My mother recorded it in my baby book as "My First Trip." As I grew up, I loved visiting the Harbesons because they had so many wonderful things to look at and we were always treated to some sweet concoction that Mrs. Harbeson pulled out of her oven. The one fascinating thing that always captured my attention in their home was a crystal clock that had golden spheres on the inside. The spheres rotated on the hour and pinged a sweet soft melody signaling the time. I coveted that clock! The thing about Mrs. Harbeson was that she would literally "give you the shirt off her back" and I knew full well that if I mentioned that I loved that clock, she would generously say, "It's yours!" So, I never let on that I really loved that clock. Grandma would have been livid had I mentioned it! She raised us to be "mannerly."

Mrs. Harbeson had a larger than life personality and was known to everyone as "Aunt Cleo." For reasons known only to her, though, my grandmother always addressed her as "Mrs. Harbeson" or "Sister Harbeson." Mrs. Harbeson single-handedly ran the lunchroom at our small school and her husband drove the school bus. If Mrs. Harbeson was expecting to have to cook a large or involved lunch, she would tell George or me to tell Grandma to come help her. So, Grandma would don her apron and catch the school bus with us the next day and report to the cafeteria. She and Mrs. Harbeson had a good time cooking and washing up the dishes in our cafeteria. It was considered a rare privilege to be asked to "wipe tables" after the lunch period was over, and I was always happy when I was chosen to do that. At our school, if there was food left over, students were welcome to go back for "seconds." I always prayed that there would be leftovers of the scrumptious chocolate oatmeal cookies, which was our dessert once a week.

In appreciation of Grandma's help, Mrs. Harbeson always sent her home with leftovers and once gave her a knife, which had "U.S." stamped on the handle. I still have that knife!

The Harbesons were members of our Baptist church. Once a year, at our church, we celebrated "Homecoming" with dinner on the ground. There would be mounds of fried chicken, bowls of potato salad, field peas and many other delicious foods. But the highlight of the long wooden table for me was Mrs. Harbeson's seven-layer chocolate cake! She never had to worry about leftovers, because there weren't any!

When Jerry and I announced our engagement, Mrs. Harbeson volunteered to make our wedding cake as her present to us. It was beautiful and very special, but it could never match the taste of her chocolate oatmeal cookies or that marvelous seven-layer chocolate cake!

THE WALDEN FAMILY

Cheryl (Walden) Gaskin has been my friend for over fifty years now and even though we live eight hundred miles apart, we are still close at heart. She is like a sister to me. We met when the Kinard School was closed, due to a lack of enrollments. We were in third grade and became fast friends at Frink School, a school about fifteen miles from Kinard.

Cheryl was the only girl in her family. She had two older brothers and one younger brother, and I learned later that there had been other siblings. Her mother, Christell, lost a son in infancy, a daughter, born with underdeveloped lungs, who lived only days, and another son, who was killed in an automobile accident. Having lost my daughter, I am still amazed at how Mrs. Walden endured her grief and is now ninety-nine years old. She is the strongest one-hundred-pound woman that I have ever met.

Cheryl and I seemed to do everything together and many times I would tell my brother, George, to tell Grandma I was spending the night at the Walden's home. Cheryl and I would get off the school bus together at her stop and walk the dirt road to her home. Usually, Mrs. Walden was out in her garden, hoeing weeds or gathering vegetables. She always seemed glad to see me, even though she had no knowledge that I was coming! Cheryl's father worked so we didn't see him until dinner, but he, too, never seemed to mind an extra person at the table. Ed, the oldest son, treated me like a sister. Danny, the next oldest, tolerated me and teasingly (I hope), called me "Sky Witch!" Sam, the baby boy, considered me the "kindest, most pretty girl he knew." He had printed these words on a picture of himself that he gave me. And so, I felt like I was part of the Walden family!

Cheryl and I found all sorts of things to entertain ourselves with, but one of my favorite activities was going "violet picking." It seems to me that we must have been gone for hours, traipsing around the woods surrounding the Walden's home, but when we did return, we both carried huge bouquets of violets for her mother. We walked to her aunt's house and visited her first cousin, Patsy. We walked to Bruton's Store, a small country store not far from Cheryl's home, owned by Mrs. Annie Bruton. Of course, we did our homework before we started out on all these adventures.

We attended Frink School until seventh grade, and then we went to Carr School in Clarksville, Florida, for seventh and eighth grade. After four years, we graduated from Blountstown High School and then from Chipola Junior College in Marianna. Cheryl and her fiancé Carlos were then married and had to move to Miami for a school year. Carlos did his internship there, teaching chemistry and Cheryl worked. Later they would move back, first to Blountstown, then to Quincy, and now Tallahassee. Somehow, Cheryl managed to work and take classes at the same time. She got her degree in English Education from Florida State University

Meanwhile, I went to the University of West Florida in Pensacola and graduated with a degree in elementary education. My brother, George, graduated a year after me and also attended UWF, but in the second year, his draft number was very low, and fearing he would be drafted, he joined the Army and was sent to Thailand, during the Vietnam War.

In my second year at UWF, I met Jerry, through his roommate, Glenn. Glenn, who is African American, was studying to be a teacher. Our literature class gave him fits, so I would help him with our assignments. He decided I should meet his roommate. We did meet and we recently celebrated our forty-ninth wedding anniversary! Thank you, Glenn! (Glenn graduated with me and became an elementary school principal.)

Cheryl, Carlos, Jerry and I, are now retired teachers and our friendship continues. I will ever be grateful to my Walden family for all the good times they gave me as I grew up.

Christell Nichols-Walden – 99 and counting!

MRS. LEILA

Mrs. Leila Shiver and her husband, Clayton, lived about three miles from us. She was my Sunday School teacher and would faithfully stop by and pick us up to go to church. Grandma reckoned as to how Mrs. Leila's mother misspelled her name since it was pronounced "Leela" not "Lee-I-La." Grandma didn't cotton to people "putting on airs and being all uppity" so she thought Mrs. Leila's mother stuck the extra "i" in her name to make it sound more refined! But, Grandma liked Mrs. Leila, anyway. The Shivers lived in a nice home with a big porch and a circular drive. Tall pines separated the house from the highway. "Aunt Sheely" as she was known to all, lived with them. She was Mr. Shiver's mother, a tiny wizened figure who rarely spoke and, yet, had a commanding presence about her.

One Easter, Mrs. Leila invited all of us in her Sunday School class for an egg hunt at her house. It was a real treat and we all found lots of eggs. She had hidden a special prize egg, which had a dollar bill taped to it and although I don't remember who found it, I know that person was thrilled. A whole dollar! Imagine! Mrs. Leila had made sugar cookies for us which we enjoyed with our eggs and the sugared Kool-Aid.

The Shivers were unable to have children of their own but adopted a little baby boy, whom they named Joe. I remember going with Mrs. Leila to pick Joe up because Mr. Shiver had to work. What a sweet tiny bundle of joy he was and I was honored to hold him while Mrs. Leila drove home. Mrs. Leila's mother and family lived in Lynn Haven, near Panama City and she would visit them about once a month. She would come by and pick me up so that I could hold Joe for the trip there and back. Joe was a very good baby and I loved being able to care of him. His grandparents truly doted on him and always had a huge spread ready for us to eat when we got there. After lunch, we would go out back, while Joe slept, and pick figs from two huge trees. I didn't like fresh figs, but I would take home my pickings to Grandma, who would turn them into delicious fig preserves.

TINY BABY GIRL

Our neighbors, the Mears family, thought their child-rearing days were over since their two sons were teenagers. But to their surprise, Mrs. Mears gave birth to a baby girl, whom they named Janet. I loved Janet dearly and found excuses to visit her daily. Mrs. Mears became pregnant again about a year later and went into labor prematurely. Our family kept Janet while Mr. Mears drove his wife to Blountstown to Dr. Snyder's clinic to have the baby. There was no hospital in Blountstown at that time and Dr. Snyder was the only doctor there. So while we waited anxiously at home with Janet, tiny Marie Mears was born weighing in at four pounds, four ounces. Although she was about six weeks premature, her features were perfect in every way. Mr. Mears came home after Marie was born and took Janet and me back to the clinic to see the tiny baby girl. She was lying swaddled in blankets in a small cubicle, with her mother resting nearby on an examining table.

Regular cloth diapers were much too big for the baby girl, so Mrs. Mears cut the diapers into quarters to fit Marie's tiny bottom. Marie's big brother, Earl, took a drawer out of his dresser and placed a folded quilt in it. Then he laid soft sheets on top of the quilt and that was Marie's bed for a long time. She finally outgrew the drawer and, in fact, grew up to be a very healthy little girl.

Sadly, Mr. and Mrs. Mears would later divorce and move away. Mr. Mears moved down to south Florida and Mrs. Mears moved to Blountstown and remarried. Alton and Earl both served in the military and Alton bought a blue Chevrolet convertible. He took George and me for a ride in it and we had a great time. Earl came home for Blountstown's Homecoming one year and George and I went with him to the game. Through Facebook, I have reconnected with the girls and will always remember the Mears' family as good neighbors. We missed their friendship after they moved away.

RUNNING FROM THE STORM

Whenever there was a hurricane in the gulf, we would have guests, who became good friends, come to stay in our cabins rather than ride out the storm in their homes on the beach. The guests would stay until the weather was permissible for them to return to their homes on the coast. The Burketts were regular guests and we enjoyed their company. There were some other families, too, but I always remember the Burkett family. Once, I was talking with Jerry's Aunt Eunice, who had lived on Port St. Joe Beach with her family of six. We were talking about scaling fish and I happened to mention how my father skinned catfish. Aunt Eunice exclaimed that he must have been the person who taught her husband, Lawrence, how to skin a catfish. She said that once a hurricane was in the gulf and her family came inland to a small fish camp to get out of the way of the storm's fury. The owner was skinning a mess of catfish and Lawrence was amazed at how easy he made it look. The owner offered to show Lawrence how to clean the catfish and Lawrence used that technique always after that. Aunt Eunice was convinced it was my father and it certainly could have been. Over the years, people running from the storm literally ended up on our doorsteps and we welcomed them with open arms. We were happy to be a shelter from the storm.

CHAPTER 6:

COMMUNITY EVENTS

CALHOUN COUNTY FAIR

The Calhoun County Fair was held every fall on the fairgrounds in Blountstown. During its two-week run, the county supplied a school bus to take us to visit the fair on the first Saturday it opened. Grandma went along to chaperone and to visit her favorite exhibit—the home economics tent which featured homemade jellies, jams, syrups, honeys and pickles.

In the animated movie of Charlotte's Web, there is a greedy rat, Templeton, who is overwhelmed by the heady and palpable sights, sounds and smells emanating from the fair. I identified with Templeton. It was almost too much to process, but we managed.

The organ music drifted through the air from the gaily decorated Merry-Go-Round filled with laughing children. The Tilt-a-Whirl spun round and round thrilling its riders. The Ferris wheel seemed to rotate in a never-ending circle skyward. Carnie hawkers called out, "Knock down a bottle! Win a prize! Only twenty-five cents!"

There was the normal fast-food for sale at different tents. Foods such as hamburgers, hot dogs, popcorn, and fries tempted us as we walked along. But, along with the aromatic fast-food, red delicious candied apples, hot boiled peanuts, and ice-cold sugar-cane sticks were also available for sale. None of these was what I wanted. I simply kept walking until I spied it–sticky, hot, cotton candy being swirled in a large drum by a smiling carnie!

We stayed at the fair, meandering here and there, booth to booth, talking excitedly about what we had seen or done, as more and more people arrived, coming in from nearby small towns, bringing excited children with them. Many of the children ran headlong, squealing with delight, while others began pleading with their parents for money to ride on the rides or buy some food.

Five hours flew by quickly, and it was time to board the yellow school bus and head home. We were tired, but happily so and knew that the fair would return next year and we could visit once again.

STONE'S STORE

M.J. Hill and his wife, Viola, owned the general store in Kinard, across the street from my elementary school. They had three daughters and a son, and by the time Mr. Hill suffered a fatal heart attack years later, the children were grown and married. One daughter, Nadine, and her husband, Ben Stone, took over the running of the store. So, it became Stone's General Store and Post Office. The store held a menagerie of items, from groceries and food items to fertilizer, fish bait, and hunting supplies. It was the only store for miles around, so everyone shopped there out of necessity but also because the Stone family was so friendly. Although we did not visit the store often because we grew our own food in our garden, we did have to shop for staples such as sugar, cornmeal, flour and cooking oil, as needed. I loved going to the store and my favorite aisle was the candy aisle and the large Coke refrigerator. I also loved the large gingerbread cookie decorated with pink icing, which they sold. For a nickel, I would buy a Coke and with another nickel, a gingerbread cookie, and then, I was in Heaven with my treats.

The Stone family was a truly generous and kind family, and they would let customers "run a tab" if they needed to do so. We had our own tab and Daddy kept it paid up.

The Stones had five children, and one year, when they were coming home from a trip late at night; Mr. Stone fell asleep at the wheel, lost control of the car, and was killed immediately from the impact. The family was all thrown from the car and injured, but they survived. It was a very sad day and week in Kinard after this tragedy happened. But, after the funeral, Nadine decided to keep the store open and going, which she did for many years. She also served as Kinard's postmistress, all the while raising her five children alone. Nadine Stone was a very strong woman, in more ways than one, and well-liked by everyone who knew her.

CHURCH

Every Sunday morning, Mrs. Leila Shiver would pick us up for church. Our tiny church had a long name—Cypress Creek Missionary Baptist Church—and everyone was greeted with a "Hello, Brother" or "Hello, Sister!" Brother Monroe Johnson led the singing. He didn't direct the music and we didn't have a choir, so he just sang along with the rest of us. His daughter-in-law, Minnie, played the piano to accompany us. I loved (and still love) the gospel songs we sang then.

The preachers we had never simply SPOKE a sermon. It wouldn't be a sermon if the preacher didn't pound the pulpit for emphasis. The messages we heard did not teach God's love and grace, but rather his mighty power and the suffering you would endure if you did not accept God as your personal savior. Hellfire and damnation was our religion. You either believed in Hell's fire or you would go there when you died.

I decided to join the church when I was eleven years old. Since we did not own a baptismal font, my baptism was held at Cypress Creek and many of the church members attended it. I was wearing one of my "church" dresses and a white plastic hairband and, as soon as I was dunked in the cold creek water, my hairband floated off downstream. I was too cold to try and retrieve it, so, the preacher and I walked toward the shore and someone, mercifully, handed me a towel.

There were only two churches in Kinard, ours and the Pentecostal church, which was closer into town than ours. Our Pentecostal friends had much stricter rules than we did at our church. They were never to cut their hair, wear make-up or nail polish and their dresses had to be extra-long, so as to show no skin. There were two things we agreed upon-only dresses were to be worn in church, no slacks or jeans, and we were not allowed to dance. Dancing was thought to be an evil practice.

Church was held on Sunday mornings and Sunday nights. Our preachers came from Panama City, which was forty miles from our church. We shared our preachers with another Baptist church which was not far away.

I don't ever remember really loving the sermons, although they were far from boring. I could never understand how some older gentlemen in our congregation seemed to nod off during the sermon. Just about the time I would think I might relax, the preacher would bang on the pulpit and jolt me upright. I went to church because that's what we did every Sunday. I loved singing, Sunday school, and spending time with my friends. When the Sunday school teacher for the primary grades moved away, I asked the deacons of the church if I could teach them and they said, "Yes." I was sixteen at that time.

POUNDINGS

Poundings were occasions brought about from necessities. When a young couple married in our small community, most of the time they didn't have all of the items needed for a well-stocked pantry.

So, the ladies of the community would hold a "pounding" for the newlyweds. Each attendee was to bring a pound of useable goods for the couple. Of course, most brought more than one pound, but the items brought ranged from sugar, flour, and cornmeal, to a pound of ten-penny nails or seeds to plant at their new home. Lots of homemade jellies, pickles and tupelo honey could be found at the poundings, which were always held at the local church. Although the young groom did not attend these "ladies only" events, I am sure he was very grateful for the generous windfall that his bride would bring home from the pounding.

HALLOWEEN CARNIVAL

Children didn't go trick-or-treating in the country. The nearest neighbor could be at least a mile or so away, making trick-or-treating last hours. Then, too, was the notion of wearing costumes. Most of us had clothes we wore daily and Sunday clothes, but no costumes. Our school filled in this absence of celebrating Halloween, by having a Halloween Carnival every year.

Booths were set up in our classrooms and the whole community turned out for the fun. Two of my favorite booths were the "Go Fish" and the "Cake Walk." The Cake Walk had real homemade cakes donated by the ladies of the community and it was a special tasty treat if you were lucky enough to win one of these. Lots of good food was housed in the cafeteria, and outside, several washtubs held ice-cold sodas. A big kettle, suspended over an open fire, boiled fresh peanuts. If it was a cold night, the fire was a good gathering place to warm up your backside, too.

Daddy set up an old bucket, had several boxes of saltine crackers, a couple bottles of Tabasco sauce, a few bowls and towels. He sat on the bucket, pulled on his work gloves and grabbed his oyster knife. To anyone wanting an oyster on the half-shell, he would reach into the iced tub of oysters and shuck a fresh one for them. He always had an audience because he could shuck the tasty seafood blindly, if need be. While he deftly shucked oysters for everyone, he managed to eat quite a few. His favorite way to eat an oyster was to scrape the oyster from its shell, place it on a saltine, douse it with Tabasco sauce and eat the whole thing in one bite.

It wasn't required to wear a costume to the carnival but many of the children did wear one because it was fun to get to pretend and dress-up. I really wanted to wear a costume but I wasn't sure just how to create one. There was a dress of dark green taffeta that hung in my mother's closet and since it would never be worn again, Grandma altered it to fit me. It made a long beautiful gown for me and I felt like I was a princess when I wore it. I still remember the soft swishing sound the dress made as I walked. I outgrew the dress quickly but not the memories.

QUILTING PARTIES

My mother loved the life she had at the fish camp but she missed getting together with her friends. She was a very outgoing person and longed for the fellowship of other ladies. The problem with getting together for a social time was two-fold. First, people did not live near each other, so getting together would entail driving to the destination. Secondly, most women worked at home, caring for their children and maintaining the gardens and fields. They had very little free time. My mother knew she would have to come up with a very good reason to get together. After watching my grandmother quilt and seeing how long it took to finish the quilt, my mother proposed a "Quilting Party" be formed. The quilting party would work this way— anyone who needed a quilt finished, would host a quilting party at her home. She would have the quilt attached to quilting frames, ladies would bring their own needles and thimbles, and quilting and gossiping would begin by about 9 a.m. Around noon, the ladies would take a break and the host would serve refreshments, usually finger foods and tea, water or coffee. After eating, back to the quilting they would go and stitch and talk until about 4 p.m. If enough members attended, the quilt would be quilted and the only thing left to do was for the host to do the fingerwork around the edges of the quilt. It was a win-win situation—everyone enjoyed visiting the others, and the host had a finished quilt to enjoy. Even if the quilters were unable to finish stitching the quilt in one sitting, the quilt would be mostly done, leaving less work for the host. Grandma always quilted with the smallest needles and made beautiful stitches on the quilts she worked on. My mother quilted too, but her talent was embroidering, which she was very good at. Grandma really tried to teach me the small stitches, but sadly, I never was able to master the technique. Finally, Grandma found something I was good at—threading her needles, so that was my job. The County Record newspaper heard of Kinard's quilting parties and did an article on the ladies, complete with a wonderful picture of them. Many lasting friendships resulted from these quilting parties and many beautiful quilts were turned out as a result. I especially enjoyed the parties when Grandma hosted because as refreshments, she made deviled eggs and peanut butter filled Ritz crackers, a real treat! Coffee and ice water were also served. We did not have tea, which I know sounds strange, but I think tea was not readily available in Grandma's Alabama home. She had a long walk to the country store for staples and tea was not high on her list. So, when she moved to Kinard, she just never thought about buying tea. We drank water, milk and coffee growing up, and my father always had coffee brewing, a habit my brother, Bill, and sister, Sarah, have carried on.

KINARD'S QUILTING CLUB

(PICTURE ORIGINALLY PUBLISHED IN THE *Calhoun County Record* NEWSPAPER)

CHAPTER 7:

SCHOOL- UNFAMILIAR TERRITORY

Because of my March birthday, I was seven years old before I started school. I was enrolled in first grade because there was no kindergarten class offered. I had no idea what to expect when my father left me in the first-grade classroom that morning. He had said that I would learn a lot of new things and make new friends.

Kinard Elementary School was housed in the original high school's gymnasium. The high school had burned to the ground years earlier and the students were re-located in Frink or Blountstown High School. Kinard's gym had sustained minimal damage from the fire and was renovated into classrooms. As you entered the school, to the left were classrooms for the third and fourth graders, and to the right were classrooms for the first and second-grade students. Bathrooms were installed farther down the hall on either side, and a cafeteria was at the very back of the building. All in all, there was very little evidence that the school had once been a gym.

My stomach churned as I walked into the large classroom full of excited children. I was led to a wooden desk covered with graffiti, with gum stuck underneath. Slowly I sat down and Daddy waved "good-bye!" I was running my hand over the gum when a girl behind me started talking very loudly.

Curiosity set in and I turned around to see what she was so excited about. Immediately, I felt a hard slap on my cheek and strong hands turning me around. The teacher had not said a word. She didn't have to. I would not have turned around again if a bomb had exploded on my desk. I got the message loud and clear, as did the other children, including Miss Loudmouth. Class started shortly after that and you could have heard a pin drop on the green-tiled floor.

If you are wondering if the slap had a negative effect on me, the answer is "No!" I didn't like the slap but I loved school. I loved the teachers, the students, recess and lunch. But most of all, I loved learning how to read. Reading opened up a whole new world for me. We read from the Alice and Jerry books, Dick and Jane came later. I loved the adventures that these two children set out on!

In second grade, my teacher was Mrs. Johnson, and I loved everything she did. She was my idol, and I decided then that I wanted to be a teacher. Yes, the school was unfamiliar territory, but I enjoyed every minute of my trip through it.

RECESS

Recess was one of my favorite times at school. All students were dismissed at the same time for recess, which meant that about sixty or so students were on the playground at the same time. There must have been a teacher on recess duty, but I don't remember seeing one. Mostly, we were on our own for close to an hour each day.

There was a large swing set underneath tall pines that held six swings. You had to be really quick and lucky to claim one of these swings. I learned how to maneuver quickly as I got older, but as a younger student, I gave way to the older children and let them swing while I found other things to do.

There was a paved blacktop with a basketball hoop and some of the boys would toss a basketball at the hoop hoping to make a bucket. The net on the hoop had long since rotted away but the hoop remained a constant source of entertainment.

The schoolhouse was elevated by several concrete blocks, making an easy entry underneath.

Underneath, there was pink sandy soil and many pieces of sparkling glass from broken discarded bottles and we would carefully pick up these pieces of glass. We would turn these sharp pieces of glass into fairy castles which would be dismantled at the end of recess. The next day, we would make new castles from the same pieces of glass.

Someone always had a set of jacks, and we would find a hard-packed area of dirt to scatter the jacks and scoop them up before the tiny pink ball dropped.

Most of us brought our marbles with us to school and either played the game of marbles or "Dropbox." Dropbox was played by using an empty shoebox or cigar box with a hole cut into the lid of the box. A player would stand over the box and attempt to drop his/her marbles into the open hole from waist-height. A successful drop-boxer would ring the hole and be rewarded by getting his own marble back plus one from the box. A loser would miss the hole and forfeit his marble.

Girls would scoop mounds and mounds of pine straw and fashion elaborate playhouses with many rooms. Dolls and toys were allowed at school, and many of us brought them to school each day to play with in our playhouses.

There was another game, played mostly by the boys, called "Stick Frog". Stick Froggers carried pocket knives and would flip these knives from waist high into the hard-packed dirt. If the knife stuck handle up, the frogger was a winner. If the knife fell over, the frogger was a loser.

Years later, the thought of elementary school students playing with broken glass and pocket knives, sends chills up my spine, but that was a different time and I don't remember anyone getting hurt doing any of these things. We were trusted enough to be allowed to enjoy recess and be creative with our games.

SUBSTITUTE TEACHER

From the first day I attended school, I knew that I wanted to someday become one of these wonderful educators. Yes, my first-grade teacher slapped my cheek on my first day of school, but when I turned around and began to listen attentively, this same teacher had my undying admiration.

I thought, '*What could be better than this? Being with a classroom full of children, eagerly listening to my every word, why, it would be a dream come true!*' So, imagine my surprise and delight, when one morning my teacher, who was also the principal of the school, asked me to go across the hall and "teach" the first and second-grade students. Their teacher had an emergency arise and she could not make it to school that morning. I was the only substitute available!

It did occur to me that I was only a year older than the second graders. Would they listen to me?

I walked across the hall and opened the door. Two dozen wiggly children, including my brother, stared back at me. I explained that their teacher could not make it to school because of an emergency and that I was going to be with them for the day. Unbelievably, no one asked a question but seemed to accept the situation good-naturedly.

My teaching consisted of writing addition and subtraction problems on the long blackboard and having the students copy and solve them on their own notebook paper. When everyone had finished, we checked their answers together. I read them several stories out of the teacher's storybook and then it was time for recess, the allotted one hour time for teachers to plan and prepare for the next day. I skipped my planning time and opted for recess with all the other children. After recess, it was lunchtime for all the students and teachers. I felt sort of strange sitting with my students instead of sitting with my classmates for lunch. But that's what their teacher did, so I thought I should do the same thing.

My teacher had stuck his head in the door several times to check on me, but I assured him that everything was fine. It was fine in that no one threw spitballs, fought over a pencil, uttered a curse word, fell out of his/her desk, refused to do what

I told them to do, vomited, or peed their pants! I know that God had sent a myriad of angels to school that day to make sure everything turned out well!

The teacher was back the next day, and she called me out into the hall to ask what size dress I wore. Since Grandma made most of my clothes, I didn't have a clue as to my dress size. The very next day the teacher came in, called me out into the hall again and this time handed me a package. She told me that the package was her gift to me for teaching her class. Upon opening the package, I found a beautiful store-bought dress, which ended up fitting me perfectly. I was very proud of that dress and wore it often, but the truth is, I loved playing the teacher and did not expect anything in return for it.

PRINCESS OF KINARD ELEMENTARY

Third grade proved to be a very interesting year for me. Not only did I get to "teach" one day, but I was also chosen to be the "Princess" of Kinard Elementary. Each elementary school in Calhoun County was asked to select a princess to ride on the Homecoming float that year. Since Blountstown was bigger than the other small towns, they were allowed two princesses. So, there were two princesses from Blountstown, one from Carr Elementary in Clarksville, Florida, one from Frink Elementary, and me from Kinard Elementary. I was excited beyond belief!

The princesses were instructed to make a dress from gold taffeta fabric which could be purchased from the clothing store in Blountstown. Grandma made my dress with bell-shaped sleeves, a scalloped hemline, a fitted waistline, and a very short, full skirt. I thought it was the most beautiful dress ever and I was so proud of it!

On the morning of the parade, we had to get there early so, while Daddy helped me find the float, George and Grandma got good spots on the parade route to view the parade. Three of the other princesses arrived at the float at the same time as Daddy and I. I couldn't help but notice that their mothers had made their dresses floor length, like real ball gowns. I could have cared less though because my dress made it much easier to maneuver around in and I quickly climbed into the flatbed trailer float, while they had to be lifted in. While they were getting settled, I noticed another girl, and as fate would have it she turned out to be my best friend Cheryl's double first cousin, Patsy Nichols. Of course, I didn't know that at that time but I wondered why she was heading toward our float. Patsy's mother had chosen to make Pat's gown out of baby blue lace and it was exquisite. But the dress was blue, not gold like ours so the float director had Patsy sit at the head of our float and we flanked her on both sides. It seemed to me that we were the princesses and Patsy was our queen. It was hot that day and it seemed to take the parade a long time to get rolling. Again, I was happy to have a short dress!

Finally, we began to move from the high school and on through the streets of Blountstown. The community had lined the streets to wave and cheer us on, and we had been instructed to smile and wave happily. I was so enthralled with everything that my smiles and waves were intermittent at best. I suppose that the people watching noticed only how happy we were to be princesses for a day. Back at the high school, we dismounted the float and returned to our families. There was a big barbecue lunch and celebration at the football field, but we didn't stay for that. It was a full day. I wore my gold taffeta dress until I outgrew it. Always, it reminded me of the day I was Princess of Kinard.

EXTREME EGG HUNT, COTTON PICKING, AND SYRUP MAKING

Mr. John Daniels lived on a farm about five miles away from us and he was also one of our school bus drivers. He was a hard-working man with a kind heart and a love for children. His own children went to school with us and at one time, he was our school bus driver. Easter was approaching and Mr. and Mrs. Daniels talked with our principal and teachers about having the whole school visit their farm for an egg hunt. Just before Easter break, all of us were loaded into Mr. Daniels' bus and driven to his farm. He and his wife must have spent hours boiling, dyeing and hiding those real chicken eggs for us to find. I can't remember how many eggs there were but we must have found them all. None of us had Easter baskets but that didn't matter. We just held the eggs in our hands and when the hunt was over, we were allowed to peel and eat them. What a treat that was and how generous and kind the Daniels were to invite us!

COTTON PICKING AND SYRUP MAKING

Mr. Daniels grew cotton on his farm and when the cotton bolls were ready to be picked, he arranged a day trip for us to his farm to help him pick cotton. Each of us was given a huge croaker sack, which was scratchy to the touch, and a cotton row to pick. The rows seemed to be endless and the hot sun bore down on us unmercifully as we toiled away. Although sweaty and tired, we managed to still have fun at picking away at the bolls and even had contests to see whose sack would be the fullest at the end of the row. Mr. Daniels paid each of us a dime, no matter how much or how little cotton was in our sacks when we got to the end of the row. The dime meant two things to me—it would buy a Coke and a gingerbread cookie at Hill's Store and I didn't have any schoolwork or homework for the day!

It seems to me that on the same day of the cotton-picking trip, Mr. Daniels invited us all back over that evening for syrup making at his farm. He had grown peanuts and had made a huge fire underneath a washtub full of peanuts which he boiled for us. We were allowed to eat the briny, hot peanuts as soon as they were scooped from the washtub. Our parents were invited to this event also, and the men especially enjoyed watching Mr. Daniel's mule grinding the sugarcane for the syrup. The mule was tied to a pole that was attached to another pole that held a covered tub of sugarcane poles. As the mule plodded away, always in a circle because he had no other choice, the sugarcane poles were ground up and their juices were retrieved to be boiled into syrup. The smell that penetrated the air of the boiling sugarcane was unbelievably sweet. This was a long process and Mr. Daniels had been at work all day so that there were some jars of beautiful brown sugarcane syrup already waiting for us to sample. He also had cut and peeled sugarcane poles and placed them in buckets of ice water, and we were allowed to choose as many as we wanted to eat. Nothing seemed to taste as good as hot, boiled peanuts, cane syrup and cold sugarcane poles.

These memories are so dear to me, as I reflect on them, because the Daniels were not rich, but they were very generous with what they had. It wasn't expected of them to be so generous—they just were! It was their kind way of getting all of us together—a rare treat—since most of these good neighbors knew that as soon as this time of socializing was over, they would return to their everyday exhausting jobs. One day following another and another and another. Life in the days of Hardscrabble!

THE WRECK

Dr. Harold Canning was Wewahitchka's only doctor and he shared hospital rounds with Dr. Grayson Snyder, Blountstown's only doctor. The hospital was located in Blountstown, so Dr. Snyder who lived in Blountstown didn't have a long way to drive. But it was a different story for Dr. Canning, who lived in Wewahitchka, about twenty-eight miles from Blountstown. Dr. Canning must have been running late this particular morning, possibly traveling at a fast speed, when all at once he crossed the bridge just as George and I were crossing the highway to get on the school bus. The bus had its red stop sign out, and George and I were paying attention to it, instead of being mindful of a car quickly approaching us.

Dr. Canning made the split-second decision to veer to the left, toward the steep ditches, to avoid hitting us. His car literally flew off the highway as we stood by helplessly and watched. Our neighbor, Mrs. Mears, heard the crash and called the sheriff. She and Grandma got to the bus at about the same time but when Grandma saw what had happened, she went back to the big house and got one of our woolen blankets to keep the doctor warm. Reflecting back, the blanket was probably used to cover up any blood we might see. Grandma, Mrs. Mears and our bus driver made sure we stayed on the bus. Several other neighbors came out to stay with Dr. Canning and keep him as comfortable as possible. The sheriff had contacted the funeral home, to use the hearse/ambulance, to meet him at the site of the wreck.

The sheriff and the ambulance driver arrived at about the same time, and Dr. Canning, who was lucid and very much concerned about our well-being instead of his own, was placed in the ambulance and taken to the hospital. His injuries were minor, which was a miracle since his car was a total wreck and had to be pulled out with a tow truck.

We were driven on to school and the wreck was the hot topic of the day. Our peers seemed to never tire of talking about how the wreck had happened.

It wasn't until years later that the realization of what could have happened really sank in for me.

I know Someone was watching over us that day!

CHAPTER 8:

FISH STORIES

THE FISHERMAN'S DAUGHTER

The fisherman's daughter sat watching her father. They had stopped the rough-hewn
wooden boat, anchoring it with a heavy red brick tossed into the inky black creek.
Sounds abounded. The water oaks rustled in the gentle breeze.
A red-headed woodpecker could be heard pecking on a nearby oak.
Somewhere the water stirred as a curious fish surfaced slyly.
A large bullfrog dove from his water-logged stump into the sanctity of the creek.
Overhead, crows cawed greetings and flew on in search of food.
The fisherman's daughter moved not a muscle for fear she would disappoint
    her father.
Her father, so much larger than life to her, managed to silence his tall frame,
As he diligently and deftly secured bait onto two cane poles.
The bait, earthworms, dug that very morning, was still very much alive.
The girl wondered if the worms sensed their fate.
The fisherman handed one of the bait-filled poles to his daughter.
Barely louder than a soft whisper, her father said,
"Cast your pole near those old logs but be careful not to get hung up."
The fisherman's daughter knew all too well that a shiny shellcracker could be hid-
    den in the rotting logs.
She knew, too, that getting "hung up" could be a costly mistake.
The fish would get away and while getting away, would tangle her line in the logs.
This would require her father's assistance to get loose.
And she could risk losing her hook, line, sinker, and cork.
Items such as these would be replaceable, but expensive. She knew full well that this
    outing was anything but playtime.
She and the fisherman were on a mission.
The mission was to catch as many fish as possible before the noonday sun beat
    down mercilessly upon them. The fish would be cleaned and frozen to eat at
    a later time.

Remembering how her father had taught her,

The girl gingerly cast her cane pole near the partially submerged rotting logs.

As luck would have it, no sooner had she cast her line, than a large horsefly bit her on her bare arm.

The fisherman's daughter screamed, jumped up and let go of her pole. Her father watched as the wooden cork disappeared under the logs. He knew that a smart fish had grabbed the bait and swam clean away.

Quickly, but silently, he snatched the floating pole,

Laid it inside the boat and took an old towel from beneath his seat.

He dipped the towel into the cold creek water

And wrapped it around his daughter's arm which was already turning red.

"Stupid old horsefly," she said, "now I'll never get that shellcracker!"

"Oh, I wouldn't be too sure of that. Never is a long time," replied the fisherman,

As he cast his cane pole near the same rotting logs.

"Let me see if I can catch that ol' shellcracker," he drawled.

As if on cue, his wooden cork dove under the water lightning fast. The fisherman held the pole steady and slowly pulled it near the boat.

His daughter watched the water churn fiercely.

The fisherman pulled the pole inward and a shiny shellcracker dangled at the end of the line. "There now. Told ya, never was a long time," her father said.

Grabbing the fish, he unhooked it and took a long look at it.

"Well, Big Feller, looks like you bit off more than you can chew this time!"

He strung the shellcracker on the rope stringer which was tied to the back of the boat

And baited his hook again.

To his daughter, he said, "Let's see if we can catch his brothers and cousins." He baited her pole and handed it to her.

This time she searched the air for any errant horseflies before she cast her line.

Seeing none, she cast near the rotting logs again.

The rest of the morning was spent in silence as the father and daughter caught a good mess of fish and completed their mission successfully.

A TRUE FISH TALE

It was not unusual for Daddy to go on an overnight fishing trip with fishermen who rented our cabins. What was unusual was that one particular time, George and I were allowed to go with these fishermen. Normally, Daddy would leave to go fishing no later than four a.m., but since this was an overnight trip, we started out after lunch. We were in two boats—Daddy, George and I were in one boat and the three guest fishermen were in the other. Our boat also carried the camping equipment and ingredients for the night's meal, the jugs of drinking water and a cooler of beer. Daddy led the way to a promising spot on the Dead Lakes where we anchored and fished. The men were unaware that Daddy had searched out this spot ahead of time and knew that it was a shellcracker bed. As soon as the men cast into the black waters of the lake, they began pulling in shellcracker, short, fat small fish, just the right size for a fish fry. When the biting lessened, Daddy led the way to yet another prime fishing hole and once again, the men had great luck. This time, bream were being caught and our live well was steadily filling up. As the day wore on, the men, mellow from the beer and the success of the fishing excursion, were more than glad when Daddy assessed that we had plenty of fish for a fish fry and we should find an appropriate campground and get the fire started. Daddy anchored and led us to a clearing in the water oaks. He sent George and me to get firewood and he started to clean the fish as the guest fishermen lounged and regaled stories of the fish they had caught, each fish got bigger as the beer expanded the men's thinking processes. George and I returned with the firewood only to find Daddy frantically searching through the foodstuffs scattered on the ground. "I know I brought it. Where is it?" Daddy asked. "Where is what?" George asked. "The grease, the cooking oil," Daddy answered.

Sure enough, after searching through the pans, the flour, the onions, eggs, and utensils, we found no grease. I don't know how Daddy did it, but he managed to cook fish and hush puppies, pork and beans, and hot brewed coffee over a campfire, and it was wonderful. The next morning, we drank coffee, carefully doused the campfire, loaded the boats and headed for our boat landing. All things considered, it was a successful trip, and the fishermen declared that they would surely return as soon as they were able. Upon entering our house, Grandma held up a gallon jug of cooking oil and said, "Did you forget something, Bill?"

SET HOOKS AND TROT LINES

Cypress Creek was a never-ending source of entertainment and food for our family. The harvesting of set hooks and trotlines provided daily surprises and fresh fish from the creek's murky waters.

Set hooks, or limb hooks, were made by attaching fishing line from a low hanging water oak. Hooked bait was on the end of the fishing line, which was submerged about three to five feet into the creek. Daddy once brought home an eight-pound bass from one of these set hooks and we were rightfully impressed. But in Daddy's drawling, unpretentious way he said, "Aw, he's just a little feller. The big one is in the boat!" Upon running to the boat, we spied an eleven-pound bass, lying in the bottom of the wooden boat!

Neither set hooks nor trot lines were legal, but lots of people fished in this way and it was a way of life. It was a way to supplement our diet, not a sport or a recreational activity. There were game wardens that patrolled the creek and the Dead Lakes, but they seemed to turn a blind eye to the set hooks and trot lines. I don't recall anyone ever getting caught for fishing with them.

Trot lines were made by stringing fishing line across the creek from one tree to another. The lines were weighted down with old bricks, cement blocks, or whatever would do the trick. The idea was to make sure that the lines would never float to the surface. On these lines, Daddy placed as many as twenty-five hooks baited with anything he thought might be attractive to the fish. Octagon soap was one thing he used, which I never understood, but it worked! Mostly, though, Daddy used bait fish to hook the naïve fish as it swam by. It was fun to "run" the trotlines because you never knew what might be on the end of the hook. Turtles sometimes were able to wreck the hooks by snatching the bait off quickly with their powerful jaws. But, other times, turtles themselves would be caught and if the turtle was edible, he would join in with the catch of the day. If he was too small, he lived to be caught another day.

To keep the set hooks and trot lines going took a lot of doing. First, they had to be baited and then they had to be checked and re-baited, so it was an ongoing process, but it proved to be an excellent way to keep us in fresh fish. And there was always the curiosity of wondering what would be caught on the hooks.

JUNIOR

Although Daddy had an outdoor fish-cleaning area near the "big house", often he would clean the fish he'd caught down at the boat landing, throwing the entrails out into the creek. One day as he was cleaning the day's catch, two green eyes appeared silently near the mouth of the landing. Daddy saw the eyes but continued to clean his fish and throw the guts into the creek. This time, though, he threw the guts further out, toward the lurking dark eyes. As soon as the entrails hit the water, the eyes disappeared from the surface with a big swishing sound and a rippling of water. The alligator gulped down the guts and then swiftly swam away. Daddy told us about his encounter with the alligator and that this was a young gator, not very large, and, apparently, not too afraid of being offered a hand-out. The next time Daddy cleaned fish, George and I went with him to see if the alligator would come for a meal. For a while, nothing happened, and then, just as Daddy had said, the eyes appeared above the surface of the water. George and I were delighted. Daddy threw some entrails toward the gator and the gator quickly dove underneath them and gobbled them down. Again, he swam away. But as this routine became regular, the gator would stay longer and nearer each time. George and I took turns throwing food his way and Daddy named the gator, "Junior." Don't get me wrong. We knew all too well that at any moment, Junior could swim up to the water's edge and head menacingly toward us. But we did not fear Junior, and it seemed the respect was mutual. He never swam close enough to really give us cause to panic and we never ventured further than the edge of the boat landing. Seeing Junior enjoy his food was enough to satisfy our need to get closer to the gator. Daddy continued to throw entrails his way, hollering, "Here, Junior!" and Junior would comply by gobbling the food down quickly. One day, Junior did not show up for his regular meal and Daddy was not too concerned, saying Junior was getting bigger and probably was hunting food for himself. But after about a week of no-shows by Junior, Daddy came home one day and said, "I found Junior!" George and I were ecstatic until slowly Daddy told us that Junior's carcass was tossed up on some cypress knees, close to where Cypress Creek met the Dead Lakes. Daddy surmised that some men out for a "good time" shot Junior and then did not take his hide since he was not a large gator. They just left him in the swamp, as if he was a useless piece of trash. But George and I knew better. Junior was and always will be a good memory of my childhood years and childhood seemed a little darker and more foreboding after Junior was killed.

DEEP SEA FISHING

Uncle George, my mother's youngest brother, came down at least once a year to go deep-sea fishing with my father. Once, Aunt Frances, my mother's sister, came with him and they decided that I was old enough to go fishing with them. What a thrill! We left the fish camp at about three o'clock in the morning in order to get to Captain Anderson's Pier in Panama City in time for the four-thirty boat departure.

The captain of the boat sped us out about thirty miles from the shore, and though the morning air was chilly, I couldn't resist standing on the bow of the boat as we navigated the gulf waters. The sun was just beginning to peek over the horizon when we anchored in the calm ocean. Since I was literally just along for the ride, I enjoyed watching everyone bait their hooks and try their luck. The deckhands busied themselves by bringing more and more B-liners (vermillion red snapper) for bait and soon the fishers began pulling in grouper and snapper. The smell of the fish mixed with the ocean air was a heady combination and not all noses were up for it. My aunt Frances was the owner of one such nose. Bless her heart! Seasickness hit her with a vengeance and she went below deck to lie down. Daddy sent me down to check on her and told me to tell her to eat one of the pimento cheese sandwiches which we had packed. I dutifully relayed the message to my poor aunt. She seemed to turn even greener at the prospect of eating a pimento cheese sandwich!

There was a "pot", into which anyone who wanted could contribute. The winner of the pot would be the person who caught the biggest fish. Daddy always baited his hook in a certain way, and he and a passenger on the other side of the boat got their lines tangled. The other fisherman claimed the grouper was his but Daddy called the captain down and showed him how the hook definitely belonged to him. It was the biggest catch of the day, so Daddy won a whopping $28.00 for his catch. Aunt Frances, who was mostly recovered by the time we docked, loved to tell Daddy's hook story, but she never found her seasickness voyage worth repeating to anyone.

SOLITARY BOAT RIDE

Gritty, dark, wet soil squished between her toes
Smells of the tupelo trees mixed with the damp swamp penetrated her nostrils.
Her heart rejoiced as she clambered into the old wooden boat.
The rough-hewn paddle in her hands, she shoved away from the shore.
Silence enveloped her, broken only by the buzzing of an occasional fly
Or the caw of a crow soaring overhead.
Cypress Creek held secrets, and the girl did not care to learn them.
She simply wanted to embrace the quietness and beauty.
Maneuvering the boat out into the slow-flowing current, the girl rested the paddle.

She sat on the boat seat and let the boat drift.

The boat was older than her ten-year-old self and water began silently seeping
In through the tiny crevices.

Bare toes relished the cool of the water as it swished beneath them
But the girl knew she'd soon have to reach for the old tin bailing can,
If she journeyed long.

The summer sun beat down upon the girl as the boat floated slowly
    and methodically,
And the girl felt not the heat, but the serenity and solace of the slow boat ride.

Suddenly, the current flowed more and more swiftly and the boat was pulled
Toward a protruding shade-covered sandbar.

Anticipating the collision, the girl stood up, bracing herself on the sides of the boat.

As the boat nudged the sandbar, the girl grabbed her paddle to steady the boat,
Lest the menacing current should sweep it away.

A retreat awaited her and she wanted to visit, so she leaped out and pulled
The anchoring knotted rope behind her.

Using all the strength her tiny body could muster, she dragged the boat securely
Onto the sandbar and tied the rope to a nearby water oak.

Plopping down with abandon now, her bare toes dug into the sand,
Not the inky, coarse, black soil of the boat landing, but sand, fine, white
    and delicate.

Something glimmered and shifted as the tide rustled the water along.

Fool's Gold kept her visiting the sandbar often.

Not valuable, it still swished and swayed riveting her undivided attention.

Growling sounds erupted from her stomach, signaling dinner on the stove
Was awaiting her at home.

Reluctantly, she untied the rough rope and climbed back into the boat.

Immediately, as she shoved off, she began to paddle furiously,
Fighting the swift current.

Traveling upstream would be a battle, in contrast to the
Slow moving trip downstream.

A veteran at conquering currents, she deftly headed the boat toward home.

As the boat slipped onto the shore at the landing, she hopped out
And knotted the rope securely, once again.

Vowing to return tomorrow, she indulged in one long-lasting look at
The quiet creek then scurried up the slight slope and ran toward home.

CHAPTER 9:

JUST FOR FUN

PLAYTIME AT THE FISHCAMP

Although George and I had regular chores, such as pulling weeds, digging worms, picking grapes, gathering firewood, cleaning the cabins, and mowing the lawn, we also had a lot of free time. Toys were few, but imagination was plentiful, so we played outside most of the time and invented games of our own.

Our main playground was the large sand bed which butted up against our house. The sand had a pinkish tint, and if one dug down deep enough, red clay could be found. We made mud pies, built sandcastles, and created frog houses for any unsuspecting frog that might hop by. Once, we took an old ball and a skinny plank, dug nine holes in the sand, and played our own version of golf. My Uncle George, always claimed that Daddy was a good golfer, but George and I just whacked away at the old ball with the skinny plank and had a good time, unconcerned about par, bogeys, birdies, eagles, or holes in one. We played softball the same way, only with a wider plank.

We found an old tire that Daddy had discarded and created "Roll the tire." The rule to play this was simple: roll the tire until it (or you) falls. There were several empty old metal barrels on the fish camp and George and I would climb one of these, stand up and "walk" the barrel from the cook shack to the big house and back again.

I always had my dolls to play with and, since George wasn't keen on playing with dolls, I was very glad to have Cheryl visit. We would dress up in my mother's clothes, carry the dolls to the cook shack and "cook" lunch for them. I don't think we had tea parties since we didn't drink tea. I'm sure we must have taken coffee breaks, instead.

The previous owners of the fish camp had run a sawmill and left a huge mountain of sawdust near the boat landing. As kids, we loved to play "King of the Mountain." We would start at the base of the sawdust pile and when the designated starter yelled, "Go!" off we'd race toward the top of the itchy, sticky sawdust pile. The first one to the top would proclaim "King!" We would retreat to the bottom and start over.

We had lots of trees to climb and I claimed one as my special reading tree, although books were scarce. I read my mother's books and Aunt Eva and Uncle George sent me a copy of Heidi. I read the book so many times that I memorized the pages.

Daddy bought us a bicycle one Christmas and we took turns learning how to ride it. We got another set of wheels from my cousin, Sharon Williams, who had outgrown her sporty, convertible turquoise Ford. It had foot pedals to power it and our bare feet pedaled them until we wore the rubber tires out.

We had shiny glass marbles and both of us were pretty good at playing marble games. I had a set of metal jacks and a ball and a jump rope fashioned from an old piece of rope that was not being used. Daddy made a tire swing for us which hung off our back porch which provided hours of entertainment.

But, of all the activities that we had in our childhood, going for a boat ride was my favorite thing to do. Growing up, I spent a lot of time enjoying boat rides.

RIPPED APART AT THE SEAMS

One summer, when I was about seven or eight years old, I went to feed our cow, Bessie, some sandspurs. I guess I thought she liked them because I wasn't really trying to be mean. I pulled some of the wicked weeds and held them out toward her and she walked slowly closer to where I was standing. So quickly I didn't even have time to blink, she lowered her head and hooked one horn into my flour-sack dress. Just as quickly, she raised her head and my dress was split in half. I fell to the ground, still holding the sandspurs, but I managed to get up and exit as fast as possible. Bessie went back to chewing her cud, never knowing she had destroyed one of my favorite dresses. I must have told Grandma what happened, and she probably mended the dress. I never offered Bessie sandspurs again!

RUNNING AWAY

One day my wanderlust got the better of me and I just walked away from home. I didn't run because it wasn't necessary. Grandma was busy and George was playing happily by himself, so I just walked away. I had about $3.00 in change and I carried it in my pocket. I just walked and walked and finally, a plan emerged—I would walk to Morgan's Store and spend my money on junk food. That is exactly what I did and then I walked back home with my junk food loot to share with George and Grandma. On the way home, Mr. Cecil McCall, a neighbor, stopped by in his pick-up truck and offered me a ride home. But I refused and walked the rest of the way home, watching his taillights disappear around the curve in the highway. My walk that day was in total about six miles and it satisfied my wanderlust for a while.

CHIPOLA PARK INN

One of the fondest memories I have is of the Chipola Park Inn, which was a beautiful Southern mansion of a hotel, located on the Dead Lakes, about three miles from our fish camp. It was owned and operated by Mr. and Mrs. Sammons and Mrs. Sammons' sister lived there and also worked at the hotel. Mr. Sammons was by trade an electrician, so he was often absent from the hotel because he was good at his trade and had a fairly large client base. The hotel was a large sprawling building with a veranda on the backside facing the Dead Lakes. Grandma, George and I paddled our boat once from our boat landing to the hotel's boat landing, tied the boat up, and walked up the slight hill to the hotel. On this particular day, Mr. Sammons was home and he saw us walking up the hill and came to meet us. He led us into the huge industrial-sized kitchen and asked if we would like a "Co-coler." I was more than delighted to accept a Coke from him, which was kept in a chest-like cooler, with the words "Coca-Cola" emblazoned on the side in red and white. Everything about the hotel fascinated me, from the beautiful veranda out back to the mahogany staircase that led to the rooms upstairs. The dining room table easily seated forty people and had silver candelabras adorning the center. The draperies were rich and dark, and rugs lay on the polished wooden floor. Besides the hotel itself, there was the boat landing and a huge shed where Mr. Sammons kept his tools and where his beautiful cocker spaniel gave birth to five puppies. When the puppies were born, he let us choose one and we chose the cute, little runt of the litter, which Daddy quickly named "Bullet." Years later, the Sammons' family graciously allowed me to hold my rehearsal dinner in their lovely dining room and as "payment" my sisters-in-law, Patricia and Shirley, polished the beautiful old candelabras until they sparkled.

Many years later, Cheryl, her mother and I went back to the graceful old building, expecting to see it in disrepair, but to our surprise, it seemed to be more beautiful than ever. A husband and wife team had bought the hotel and turned it into Covenant House, a place where people down on their luck, for any number of reasons, can live and work together as a family. The day we visited, the residents were shelling field peas and shucking ears of corn. About two dozen or so people were working and visiting with each other. The owners showed us around and invited us to come by any time. The old hotel is still making fond memories.

BULLET

Mr. Sammons owned Chipola Park Inn, a beautiful two-story hotel, about three miles by car from our house. By boat, the trip to the hotel seemed much longer, but always worth the journey. The hotel was magnificent in its heyday and still exists as a refuge for the individuals who make it their home now. The hotel had eight rooms upstairs which could be rented out to guests. The downstairs area held sleeping quarters for the Sammons family, an immense dining hall, a very large and comfortable living room, and an impressive kitchen area. The dining hall boasted a polished mahogany table with twenty-four matching chairs. A beautiful crystal chandelier hung above the massive table and silver candelabras held candles lit to help illuminate the area. Vases of porcelain held azaleas, magnolia blossoms or gardenia, depending on when the flowers bloomed. The kitchen always fascinated me with dozens of large pots and pans suspended on a rack anchored to the ceiling, huge freezers and refrigerators and a Coca-Cola cooler.

Mr. Sammon also added a garage that never served as a garage but was a great tool shed and a wonderful place for Mr. Sammons' beautiful golden Cocker Spaniel to have her five rambunctious pups. These wiggly babies were purebred cocker spaniels and Mr. Sammons could have sold them and made a profit from the sales. But, in his generosity, he allowed us to choose a pup for free. We chose the "runt" of the litter, the smallest of the five golden pups. Bullet became her name because Daddy said she was as "fast as a bullet!"

Bullet grew and thrived and was a great playmate for George and me. She was a smart dog, too, and knew when Daddy got his gun, from the homemade gun rack, that he was going hunting and she was welcome to tag along. She wasn't a hunting dog, but she loved the adventure of the hunt and when they returned and Daddy would display the rabbits or squirrels he'd killed, Bullet seemed as proud of them as Daddy was.

Bullet was not a house dog but she could be counted on to be around at feeding time, otherwise, she was off on some adventure of her own. One evening Bullet didn't show up at all and we feared that something awful had happened to her. Daddy left to look for her and came back carrying Bullet's beautiful golden body in his arms. Her face was badly swollen and Daddy reckoned that a rattler had bitten her and she had been too weak to make it home. We buried Bullet at the far end of our yard and grieved the loss of our faithful companion who had brought us so much happiness in the short time she was with us.

WHISKEY JUGS

George and his friends were used to diving in Cypress Creek, among the water moccasins, weeds, and low hanging branches of the water oaks. Looking back now, I am amazed that they never got bitten by a snake or hung up in the tree roots and drowned. No, not only did they survive, they sometimes found salvageable treasures on the creek's bottom. I have two of these treasures at my home. They are whiskey jugs in perfect condition that probably date back to the early 1900s.

Moonshining was a lucrative business in Kinard and surrounding areas, where most people farmed, worked as loggers, ran sawmills or tapped turpentine to sell. Men would set up primitive stills on the creek banks, hidden well by the large water oaks and brew moonshine which would be sold on the black market to buyers from other counties. The men had to be careful not to be caught by the "revenoors" since this would mean a stint in jail. So, my whiskey jugs are kind of a special relic of yesteryear and I treasure them.

CHERYL, THE FORD, AND I

The urge to drive hits early when you live so far away from friends that the only way to visit them is to be driven there by someone. So, when I found out that my friend, Cheryl, had learned to drive, I began to beg my father to teach me. He always found excellent excuses not to teach me, "You're too young," "You don't have a license," "I can't right now because I'm busy," all reasonable excuses, but they didn't deter me. One day, my friend, Cheryl, and I decided on a scheme that just might work. I might mention that at that time, we were in seventh grade, around twelve years old or so.

The plan was that Cheryl would spend the weekend with me and, hopefully, Daddy would get up early Saturday morning to fish and usually would be gone until dusk, giving us plenty of time to practice driving.

Everything seemed to work out in our favor. Daddy picked up a job to guide a guest for a day of fishing on the Dead Lakes. Grandma was going to work in her beloved flower bed, pulling weeds and watering as necessary. That left my brother, George, who had no clue about our little scheme, and didn't want to do girl stuff with Cheryl and me. Perfect! The stage was set! I grabbed the key of the old green Ford sedan and we were in business. Cheryl managed to crank the Ford and I rode shotgun, paying attention to everything Cheryl did. She put the car in gear, and we rolled forward. I sat mesmerized for about a minute. That was when the car simply stalled out, halfway down the partially paved driveway. No amount of coaxing would get the engine to turn over, so Cheryl put the car in park, and not knowing what else to do, we both bailed. I took the key and put it back in its place and then came the hard part—waiting for Daddy to get home and find out what we had done. Grandma had no words of comfort or aggravation. She simply shook her head and said, "Y'all shouldn't have done that!"

We had to wait quite a long while because evidently, Daddy and his guest were having a very successful fishing trip. Paying guests usually fished only for the sport of it, something that was hard for me to understand because we ate what we caught. The guest sometimes would keep his catch, but more often than not, he would donate the fish back to Daddy. Finally, we saw Daddy trudging up the hill with his string of fish. He took the fish to the cleaning area and put them down. Then, he turned to us and asked what the car was doing parked half-way down the driveway. I explained and told him it was my idea, not Cheryl's. Bless her heart, she stood right beside me the whole miserable time. Daddy didn't say a word, he just got the key and cranked the car, which miraculously sprang to life, and parked it back in its normal parking spot. The incident was never mentioned again.

Years later my brother, George, taught me how to drive. He was a very patient teacher and I appreciated him for this. His patience was severely tested when I accidentally hit a quail and killed it. I lamented hitting the quail and George remarked dryly, "Well if you hadn't been doing 85, the quail might have had a chance!"

MR. AND MRS. CARLOS GASKIN

My best friend, Cheryl Walden in 1957

OUR OWN FORD

My cousins, J.C. and Faye Williams and their daughter, Sharon, once lived in Wewahitchka, and during one trip to take Momma for another diagnosis or treatment, Daddy stopped by to visit them.

Sharon was a few years older than me and had outgrown a child's ride-in car. It was a sporty turquoise Ford car and had foot pedals to power it. J.C. and Faye gave it to my parents for George and me. When Daddy got home with Momma and began to unload the car, George and I were ecstatic! Our own Ford! We took turns driving the car up and down the sandy driveway. The car entertained us for a long time, long enough for us to wear the wheels out and then we parked it forever. Even wheel-less, the car was a catalyst for my imagination. I would put my dolls in the driver's seat and drive them off on exciting adventures.

Sadly, Sharon would become sick with tuberculosis and she and her parents moved to Arizona so that Sharon could be in a drier climate. The drier Arizona air made breathing easier for Sharon. She eventually overcame her illness and married. Unfortunately, she would later develop cancer and though she and her mother made the trip for treatments at M.D. Anderson Hospital in Houston, the cancer spread quickly and Sharon passed away in her early thirties. I can only hope that she knew how much joy she gave when she gave us the sporty little Ford.

BIRTHDAY PARTIES

When I was two years old, Momma gave me a birthday party in the front yard of our home. Birthday parties were not given back then since it was a frivolous activity, so Momma was a trendsetter of sorts. She invited Sam and Jerry McClellan, sons of Marie McClellan, one of my mother's friends. I had a pretty cake and a new dress, probably made from flour sacks. We drank Kool-Aid made from syrup and flavored with our own sugar. It was a real treat! Sam and I were the same age, but Jerry was a couple of years older. Sam and I met again years later as we entered high school and then graduated from high school together. His mother, Marie, was the daughter of Cleo Harbeson, who at one time lived across the creek from us, the only other near neighbor, besides the Mears family who lived up the hill.

As I said, my mother was a trendsetter by giving me a birthday party. Parties just weren't done because the monotony of everyday life simply didn't permit such luxuries. But, a few years later, when I entered elementary school, Brian Hill's mother threw a birthday party for him, and George and I were invited.

Brian's grandfather, M.J. Hill, owned Hill's Store, and Daddy drove us there to get a present for Brian. Hill's Store was always a marvel to me because one could buy everything from groceries to fertilizer in the place. They even carried clothing, not a huge selection, but good quality and reasonably priced.

Grandma chose a cap and a pair of shorts for Brian, which we wrapped in newspapers and took to his party. Brian, like most young boys, really was not thrilled with clothes, preferring the toys, of course. I was mortified and his mother was not happy with Brian. We did enjoy the party, though, and later I was happy to see that Brian did wear the cap and shorts, probably at his mother's insistence!

SWIMMING IN CYPRESS CREEK

My brother, George, and neighbors Alton and Earl, regularly swam in the inky blackness of the swift currents of Cypress Creek in front of the opening to our boat landing. They'd paddle out in one of our wooden boats, throw the anchor in, and take turns diving off the bow of the boat into the cold waters of the creek. They had no masks but managed to find items on the bottom of the creek and would either keep these or throw them away depending on what their perceived value was.

I was never invited to join the boys swimming in the creek. To be honest, I really wasn't too upset since I had no desire to swim out into the strong currents. However, on this particularly hot summer day, I decided to put on my hand-me-down swimsuit and swim around in the boat landing area. The shock of the cold water on my feet caused me to pause and wonder if I was doing the right thing. But, I had to admit; the water cooled my body and felt so refreshing. I drifted over to the two remaining boats, like the boys. Suddenly I saw a rippling motion and caught the tail end of a huge black water moccasin slipping into the water!

My reaction was immediate! Luckily, I was only in waist-deep water, so I ran sloshing, splashing and screaming till I got to the steep slope of our boat landing. I flopped down on the grass and that was when I saw them. Leeches! I was covered with them from head to foot. I screamed for help and saw George and Earl heading my way.

When the boys reached where I was, they started pulling the slimy blood-sucking animals off me.

I do not think I ever swam in Cypress Creek at our boat landing again. But I loved to paddle out into the currents and drift along with a baited hook and high hopes of catching a fish. Cypress Creek swimming was best left to the experts: George, Alton, Earl and the water moccasins!

THE SAWDUST PILE

Down beside the creek at the end of our land was a huge (as I remember it) sawdust pile. The former owners had run a sawmill and the end result was a twelve-foot tall sawdust hill which served as a constant playground for George, Alton, Earl, myself and Cheryl, when she came home with me. We would play "King of the Mountain" or simply just dig into the sticky sawdust and build woodchip castles, until we were thoroughly covered in sawdust. The sawdust was not easily brushed away, either. As I mentioned, it was sticky and itchy. But that never deterred us from playing in it. The sawdust pile isn't there anymore. I suppose over the years the sawdust eroded away but it remains a good memory of my childhood times for me.

BARN FIRE

We had an old shed which stood near the big house where Daddy stored a myriad of garden tools: plows, shovels, hoes, rakes, etc. But we did not have a barn and did not need one, anyway. The Mears family, our nearest neighbors, had a large barn in which they stored fertilizers, tools, and items needed for their garden. They also kept their John Deere tractor parked inside their barn. One night, we saw flames coming from the hill the Mears lived on, and we hurried up to see if we could be of help. The large barn was totally engulfed in flames licking skyward, so all we could do was form an assembly line of sorts, passing buckets of water to be doused on any sparks which might be headed toward the Mears' home. The sight of the John Deere tractor going up in flames was a terrible blow to the family. It meant that Mr. Mears, who always planted a large garden, would have to rely on a push plow to till the land. It would take a much longer time to get the garden ready without the use of the tractor. All this time, I had thought that the youngest son, Earl, was responsible for the barn fire catastrophe since he admitted to playing with matches. George told me recently that he and Earl indeed had matches but they weren't playing with them. They were igniting Cherry Bombs, little red fireworks, which made a loud noise and burst into flames! (Not so much fun!)

SELLING PEACHES

Every summer, our neighbor, Everett Mears, would travel to Georgia in his pickup truck and drive it home, filled with peaches. Before the births of her daughters, Janet and Elaine, Mrs. Mears and I would peddle the peaches around the neighborhood and even drove all the way to Port St. Joe trying to sell the pungent fruits. We met some wonderful people and most of them willingly bought the peaches which were ripe and fresh. It was a super treat for me because I missed the friends at school and I grew tired of hanging around the house in the summer. It usually meant getting to drink an ice-cold Coke from a local grocery store and that was special, too. Mrs. Mears and I always found a lot to talk about and though the weather was unbearably hot, the day seemed to pass quickly, as we rode along, stopping every so often to sell a sack of peaches.

MEXICO BEACH

Mexico Beach was about forty miles from our fish camp and when we got the chance to travel there, it was a real treat. My mother loved the beach and when any of our relatives came for a visit, Momma would plan a trip to Mexico Beach. Daddy would pick the largest watermelon, Momma took care of the sandwiches or fried chicken and potato salad for lunch, and Grandma would pack a gallon of ice water and grab towels and a big quilt for sitting on, and we'd all pile in for a trip to the beach.

To get to Mexico Beach, we would travel through Wewahitchka and make a right turn onto Overstreet Highway. Once we got to the community of Overstreet, there was a swinging bridge over the Intercoastal Waterway. If a ship or barge was coming, traffic would be stopped while the bridge swung open to let them pass. As we watched, sweating in the crowded, un-air-conditioned car, we marveled at the ship or barge as it navigated through the narrow passage. The bridge would close and lock in place after the ship or barge got through and we would be able to continue on our way. As we traveled on to White City, we could be halted once again by a suspended drawbridge. The drawbridge would open its gaping mouth to allow a ship or barge to chug through. As we enjoyed the sight, Daddy would probably be annoyed at having to wait for the whole process to be completed, but he never complained.

We always knew that we were getting close to the beach, when we saw the lighthouse at Beacon Hill. It wasn't a real lighthouse; just an addition on the roof of a house made to look like one. As soon as we saw it, we knew that straight ahead was the sparkling Gulf of Mexico. Driving on the slightly inclined street, gave one the illusion of driving straight into the gulf's waters. Reaching the highway, we made a right turn toward Mexico Beach. A left turn would have taken us to Port St. Joe, a small coastal town about five miles away. As we drove along, the Gulf seemed to take on a life of its own. Foamy white waves burst onto the pristine white sands of the beach. Then, as quickly, the water would recede, uncovering many tiny shells, called periwinkles. These jewel-like tiny shells make a wonderful stew, so I've been told. That never crossed my mind. I was just fascinated by how the waters uncovered them and gave the illusion of thousands of gems scattered along the beach.

Soon, we would reach our destination. Mexico Beach was not a big place but it was paradise to me. Green concrete picnic tables and benches, an outdoor bath house, and grills for cook-outs were what we saw as we parked. Everything we needed for a day at the beach was provided there for us, free of charge. Daddy would usually go ahead and select a picnic spot. Then, while the adults took care of choosing a table to put our picnic lunch on, George and I would rush off, barefoot, toward the beach. Barefoot was always a mistake and we always made the same mistake, never remembering the lesson we should have learned from previous beach excursions. To get to the beach, we had to cross the wickedly hot blacktopped highway. There was no reprieve for our burning feet yet because we had to make our way past through the side oats grama grass, palmetto fronds, and prickly sandspurs. Finally, we would reach the water's edge and cool our aching feet. Lots of people sat underneath brightly colored umbrellas, watching their children play. Around noon, Daddy would call us and we would hurry into the bathhouse to shower off the sand. The picnic supplies were exactly where we had left them. No one bothered them. We had our noontime meal and then Daddy would take the watermelon and slice it for dessert. Cold and crisp, it would be the perfect ending of a perfect day. As soon as we started home, George and I would fall asleep and I imagined we dreamed of the next time we could visit Mexico Beach.

GRANDDADDY CATE, MOMMA, GEORGE, AND I AT
MEXICO BEACH CIRCA ~ 1953

PEYTON AND JADEN CORE PLAYING ON MEXICO BEACH ~2015

MEXICO BEACH AFTER HURRICANE MICHAEL 2018

CHAPTER 10:

DEATHS: A PART OF LIFE

Hardscrabble! That's the best way to describe how I grew up. We were poor but I did not know it until I reached high school and saw what some of the "town kids" had. I had never thought we were poor since everyone we knew was really in the same boat as us.

Hardscrabble. That's what it was like growing up because we endured deaths as a part of life there on the fish camp. I remember the deaths of three young children that will forever be etched into my memory.

The first death I recall was that of one of our neighbor's young son. The family was gathered on the wide front porch of their home during a frightening thunderstorm, a practice not unusual, since homes were not air-conditioned at the time, and sitting on the porch provided not only a cool breeze, but the farmers had the satisfaction of watching the rain nourish their planted crops. Tragically, on this particular day, lightning struck and killed the young boy, as his family watched in horror.

A classmate of mine was saddened to learn that her younger brother had passed away. The boy had been missing for a few hours and was discovered, unresponsive, by his family. He had suffered electrocution because he accidentally fell into their electric fence, located behind their home, while standing in wet, boggy mud.

Another family lost a son, a son who was old enough to operate a mowing machine—the kind that was pulled behind a tractor. He was mowing a large pasture near Wewahitchka when the tractor hit a hole, throwing the boy off the tractor and underneath the mower. Nothing could be done to save him.

For so small a community, it seemed tragedy struck very often. Two young boys, in separate accidents, were severely burned, and though, thankfully, each lived, their recovery was long and painful.

There were more deaths later on—George lost a classmate in a log truck accident and I lost a classmate in a car wreck. I felt it necessary to mention these deaths, because our town was so small, that when someone died, neighbors came from all around to help comfort the grieving families. We had funerals and burials as a way of life in our small community. It was considered a sign of care and respect to attend the

85

funerals and so, most people made funerals a priority and would be present at these remembrance services.

A VAGUE MEMORY

Somewhere in the fuzzy deep recesses of my mind, there is a memory of a suicide that occurred many years ago. We didn't get to visit Grandma's former home very often, because travel was expensive and Mentone, Alabama, was a long way from Kinard, Florida. But, when we were fortunate enough to visit her home, we always made the rounds to see Grandma's old friends. One of these special families owned a big ranch house and raised horses, which they always allowed George and me to ride. Such a treat it was to mount and ride those magnificent animals! We always anticipated seeing this family every year, but about the time I was to enter junior high school, we made the trip to Mentone but for reasons unknown, we did not visit this family. This was very unusual since this family was very close friends and neighbors to Grandma. I had forgotten about the visit until many months later when I was reading a story about a horse and it brought back happy memories of riding horses at the Alabama's friend's home. So then, I asked my grandmother why we didn't visit these good friends.

Reluctantly, Grandma explained that these neighbors had a beautiful older daughter (Yes, I remembered her) who was in love with a boy her parents didn't like. One night, the girl took down a shotgun from the wooden gun rack and ended her life. Suicide was not a subject discussed back then, and I believe it was a heavy burden to bear for the loved ones left behind. The next time we visited Grandma's home, we did go to this neighbor's home and we were warmly greeted. Everything seemed normal, except that the girl's name was not mentioned. It felt like the elephant in the room. I'm certain that her parents grieved the rest of their earthly life. Such an incomprehensible tragedy.

A DIFFERENT REMEMBRANCE

When Mr. M.J. Hill passed away, his funeral was different. Mr. Hill was a kind, jovial man, and he had made his wife and children promise not to grieve at his funeral. To abide by his wishes, we were asked to wear brightly colored clothing, not the usual somber black that was typically worn at funerals. I remember there was a lot of laughter at the service, so I think Mr. Hill would have been pleased.

Nowadays, the service is often called "A Celebration of Life," instead of a funeral, and fond remembrances are shared by all. I think Mr. Hill was ahead of his time in his way of thinking! We celebrated Candy's life and shared some of her stellar moments at her service. She would have loved it except for one thing—she would have told me to add more flowers and decorations!

CHAPTER 11:

A DIFFERENT TIME

It was a different time.

A time—a time almost frozen in movement.

A time when neighbors checked on other neighbors.

A time when doors were left unlocked and windows were left open at night.

A time when food came from the garden, the creek and the woods.

A time when the only grocery store not only carried food,

But also for sale were clothes, cattle feed, plant seeds, and more.

It was a time when the grocery store also housed the post office.

If you needed to mail a letter from home but had no stamp, No problem.

You simply counted out the number of coins needed for the stamp,

And put them in the mailbox with the letter.

The mailman would see to it that your letter was sent along its way.

One of the best things available at the grocery store

Was meeting friends and catching up on the local news,

Not in a hurried way, just friendly back and forth banter.

It was a time when you could put your groceries on "a tab"

Until the next paycheck came in.

No one was ever turned away and no one was ever sent a bill.

Your good name and character were all that was required until payday.

Paydays came from working long tiring days of "logging"

In all kinds of woods and swamps,

Hauling the logs to the paper mill,

And returning for another load.

Others raised crops or had livestock for their income.

People shared their good fortunes by having get-togethers.

Get-togethers were dinners on the ground at the church,

Peanut boilings, cane syrup makings, hog slaughterings, or fish fries.

The ladies got together and quilted beautiful patchwork quilts.

Young married couples were treated to "Poundings!"

Poundings were usually done at the church;

The idea was to give the bride and groom a pound of items
Needed in the house—a pound of sugar, a pound of flour,
A pound of coffee, even a pound of ten-penny nails.
It was a time to sit on the porch and shell peas or beans,
Shuck corn, swat flies and mosquitos,
Pray for rain and a cooling breeze,
Wonder how your friends are faring,
Listen to the birds
Watch the butterflies gather nectar from flowers.
It was a different time.
It was a time of hardscrabble and feather beds.

EPILOGUE

I would be remiss in my storytelling if I didn't mention what my childhood home and surrounding areas look like today. Gone are the big house, the cabins, and all the other buildings that formed Cypress Creek Lodge. Replacing these are stately pines, miraculously spared from Hurricane Michael's wrath, and the home of the current owner of the property.

On October 10, 2018, Hurricane Michael, packing winds of 160 miles an hour, made landfall almost directly between Mexico Beach and Tyndall Air Force Base. A category 5 hurricane, Michael left a wide encompassing path of devastation in its wake.

Mexico Beach, which held such wonderful memories for me was left a ghost town as was Tyndall Air Force Base. Michael destroyed many businesses and homes in Panama City and then traveled on to Wewahitchka, Kinard, Clarksville, Frink, Altha, Blountstown and the surrounding communities, wreaking havoc with its high winds.

Chipola Park Inn, which used to be hidden from sight by groves of tall pines, was laid bare as Michael swept the pines away. Thankfully, the Inn was spared, having very little damage done. The owners have already begun growing new pines.

Many of these hard-working people of Northwest Florida (the Panhandle), lost their income as Michael downed trees which could have been sold, but now lie rotting in the dirt.

I felt this had to be told because these wonderful people helped raise me and I am forever grateful to all. I was blessed to know these people and know that they are rebuilding, one step at a time. I would like to thank each one, personally, but that doesn't seem possible. They will be forever stored in my memory bank of Hardscrabble Days.

(Clockwise from top left):

My brother, Bill McNew, and his wife, Robin
My brother, George McNew, with his wife, Sandra.
My sister, Sarah Dees, with husband, Bruce.

My son, Jerrod Core, with his wife, Ashley, and my
grandchildren, Peyton Elise and Jaden Austin.

MR. AND MRS. JERRY CORE ON OUR WEDDING DAY JUNE 19, 1971,
AND A RECENT PICTURE OF US.

Post Script:

No longer do I live in Hardscrabble Days. No longer do I sleep on a Feather Bed. Memories whisper and beckon me back, but I can now file them away to remember and cherish forever.